पुरातत्त्व
PURĀTATTVA

Bulletin of the Indian Archaeological Society

No. 3 1969-70

Editor
A.K. Narain

Assistant Editors
P.C. Pant
P. Singh

D.K. Printworld (P) Ltd.
New Delhi

Cataloging in Publication Data — DK
[Courtesy : D.K. Agencies (P) Ltd. <docinfo@dkagencies.com>]

Purātattva : bulletin of the Indian Archaeological Society, no. 3, 1969-70 / editor, A.K. Narain ; assistant editors, P.C. Pant, P. Singh.
p. cm.
Includes bibliographical references.
ISBN 8124602794

1. Archaeology — India — Periodicals. 2. India — Antiquities — Periodicals. 3. India — Civilization — Periodicals. I. Narain, A.K. II. Indian Archaeological Society.

First Reprinted in 2005
ISBN 81-246-0279-4
Price for volume 3 (1969-70): Rs. 600 US $ 30

Reprint authorised by
Indian Archaeological Society
New Delhi - 110 016

The Editors are not responsible for the opinions expressed by the Contributors.

Purātattva is published annually.

Manuscripts (whether in the form of articles or notes or book reviews) offered for publication should be sent to the Editor, Purātattva, Indian Archaeological Society, B-17, Qutab Institutional Area, New Delhi - 110 016.

Published and printed by:
D.K. Printworld (P) Ltd.
'*Srikunj*,' F-52, Bali Nagar
New Delhi – 110015
Phone : (011) 2545 3975, 2546 6019 Fax : (011) 2546 5926
E-mail : dkprintworld@vsnl.net
www. dkprintworld.com

CONTENTS

Status of Barley in Indian Archaeobotany with Remarks on the Aryan Hypothesis

by VISHNU-MITTRE

Wheat, barley, rice, millets and maize comprise the cereals so far discovered from the Indian archaeological sites [1]. In proportion wheat, rice and millets abound in several archaeological sites suggesting that these comprised the staple diet of the ancient Indians. Records of barley are not only scarce but are represented by few grains. *Hordeum vulgare* var. *nudum* is known from Mohenjo-Daro, and *H.* var. *hexastictum* from Harappa. Kalibangan is the only site where abundance of barley is noted in the material under examination. These three sites belong to the Harappan culture, the time spread for which is now determined between 2300 B.C.—1750 B.C. [2]. The Mohenjo-Daro charred grains are dated to 1650 B. C.[3] but the grains from other sites are not precisely dated. That the Harappan culture was not characterised by a staple diet comprising exclusively or predominantly of barley is quite clear except from Kalibangan. Further at Lothal only rice has so far been found.

Much after the decline of the Harappan culture, barley appears at Atranjikhera dated to about 1000 B.C. [4]. Its proportion at this site is not known to the author. Hitherto there is no record from the Chalcolithic period and the gap extends over 600 years.

Towards the beginning of the Christian Era barley is met with in small proportions at Ter, Osmanabad, Maharashtra [5]. Two dates 2045$\pm$100 and 1645$\pm$100 are available from this site [6].

From the above records the discontinuity in the history of barley in India is apparent more particularly during the Chalcolithic i. e. 1600 B.C. to 1100 B.C., and equally apparent is the scarcity of records from the Harappan culture except from Kalibangan. Apart from that the evidence of barley exclusively as staple diet is almost lacking except at Kalibangan. Its emergence during the Iron Age and thereafter during the early Christian Era is interesting but in proportion it is poor. On the whole the present knowledge of the ancient plant economy as built up from archaeobotanical records is not suggestive of barley as staple diet (except at a single site : Kalibangan) at any time in our history [7]. What future discoveries may have in store in this connection is yet to be seen.

In the ancient written records [8] '*Yava*' (interpreted as barley by all scholars) is so frequently mentioned that it seems to be an important article of food and comprising staple diet. The *Rik Samhita* only refers to barley and no other cereal. In the later *Samhitas* both rice and barley are prominent though wheat is also mentioned but it seems secondary. During the period of the *Upanishads* and the *Sutras* rice and barley continue to comprise staple diet and wheat finds rare mention.

Thus the literary records do not seem to corroborate the information from the archaeobotanical finds. Unless the future records change the position of the history of barley in India, one may be inclined to believe that hitherto archaeobotanical researches have brought out the plant economy of the Pre-Aryans and of the tribes contemporary with Aryans. The significance of abundance of barley at Kalibangan is to be assessed in the light of other evidences. But the presence of wheat together with barley, the age of the site and its Harappan culture preclude the possibilities of any Aryan context.

From other grounds, the Banas culture has been suggested as representing a later wave of the Aryans [9] but plant economy at Ahar, Rajasthan, comprising rice and *Sorghum*, is much different from the staple diet comprising barley or barley and rice as known from literature. The early wave of the Aryans also remains unrecognisable from archaeobotanical view-point. It is not clear if the small proportion of barley at some Harappan sites and in some Iron Age and later sites indicates indirectly the influence of the Aryan waves or barley was a constituent of the diet of pre-Aryan and later tribes. It is interesting to note in this connection that the plant economy of the Pre-Harappan cultures in Afghanistan [10] as known from Mundigak, Period II (2530 B.C.) comprised wheat only while at Deh Morasi Ghundai it comprised *Hordeum vulgare* var. *afghana* and *Aegilops tauschii*, a progenitor of wheat. This site about 60 km. northeast of Mundigak is dated to 3000 B. C. on comparative grounds.

Thus, considered purely from the archaeobotanical viewpoint, the researches hitherto done do not throw much light on the advent of Aryans in one or several waves. If barley is to be associated with them as our ancient literature suggests, then the evidence exists of the Aryan influence on indigenous cultures provided it is proven that barley was not at all a favourite cereal in ancient India prior to the arrival of the Aryans.

Notes

[1] Vishnu-Mittre, 'Protohistoric Records of Agriculture in Ancient India' *J. C. Bose Endowment Lecture* 1968, *Trans. Bose Res. Instt., Calcutta*, (in press).

[2] D. P. Agrawal, *Science*, 143, No. 3609, 1964, 950–952.

[3] *Radio-Carbon*, 1964, 231.

[4] Vishnu-Mittre, *op. cit.* [1]

[5] *Ibid.*

[6] Personal communication from Dr. Moreshwar G. Dikshit, Director of Archives and Archaeology, Maharashtra State.

[7] Vishnu-Mittre, *op cit.* [1].

[8] The History and Culture of the Indian people : *The Vedic Age*, Bharati Vidya Bhawan, (Bombay), 1965.

[9] D. P. Agrawal. *Curr. Sci.* 35, (5), 1966, 114.

[10] Bridget and Raymond Allchin, *The Birth of Indian Civilization*, Pelican Books, 1968, 258. K. A. Chowdhury, *Anthropological Papers*, 50, Pt. 2, 1963, 126-131.

Copper Red Glasses Through The Ages

by H. C. BHARDWAJ

Introduction

In fourth millennium B. C. glaze was used by the Badarians in Old Egypt and by the Jamdet Nasr people in Mesopotamia. The main purpose of the earliest glazes and glasses was to make immitation of precious and semi-precious stones for beads, amulets and inlay in jewellery. Red colour had always occupied important position in man's choice. Accordingly red jasper (an impure, opaque and compact variety of silica, coloured by iron compounds), red coral (an impure calcium carbonate in the form of skeleton of various marine organisms) and carnelian (translucent red chalcedony) were particularly used in ancient civilizations of Egypt, Mesopotamia and India.

Among the earliest red glasses (copper-red) are the specimens of beads from Ur (British Museum No. 116582) datable to circa 1800 B. C. Mesopotamian Cuneiform text of circa 1700 B. C. also mentions Akkadian Santu (red) glass. A number of glass objects of red (haematinon) colour are known from XVIII Dynasty Egypt datable to circa 1400 B. C. Since this remote antiquity and upto modern times copper red glasses have been continuously made and used. Neuberg[1] states that during the course of centuries the process of making this glass was repeatedly forgotten to be discovered afresh.

Occurrence of red glass in ancient India

No true glass has been reported from the earliest Indian civilization, e. g. Harappan cultures (datable to 2350 B. C.), but faience (glazed siliceous ware) and glazed pottery has been reported from this civilization. Among the faience objects are the chocolate coloured material, in which cuprous oxide is the colouring agent. The chemical composition of this object is reported in Table II, Sr. No. 1.

True glass specimens of copper red glass are from later archaeological sites e. g. Rajghat (Varanasi), Kausambi, Ahichchhatra, Taxila. Nasik, Kaundinyapur, (Vidarbha), Vaisali, Tripuri, Nevasa, Maski, Arikamedu, Sulur, Nalanda, some sites from Assam and quite a few other locations[2].

Dates of Indian copper red glasses

Except the chocolate red faience material which is datable to 2350 B. C., (which may be the earliest example of use of cuprous oxide as a colouring agent in glaze), the other samples are quite late. The specimens from Rajghat, Kausambi, Ahichchhatra, Taxila, Nasik are datable between 600 B. C.—200 B. C. The others belong to early centuries of the Christian era. Some of these are from unstratified deposits and hence no definite dates can be assigned.

Physical nature of this glass

The glass samples are mostly opaque, having shades of lac, jasper, coral, vermillion, cherry, burnt sienna and rarely orange. The surface is neither very smooth nor very shining, it is rather dull. However, freshly broken surfaces are lustrous.

Nature of glass objects

Amongst the objects are the beads, ear reels, thin drawn strips of haematinum (Taxila), reefs (coral like), and long unevenly cut canes (Arikamedu).

Weathering product of this glass

Excavation at Kaundinyapur (Vidarbha) has yeilded an ear re l of opaque vermillion red glass, the surface of which is covered with a mm. thick layer of green patination, a characteristic weathering product of copper. A few specimens of red glass have devitrified.

Chemical composition of ancient red glasses

Amongst the earliest example of red glazed material is from Mohenjodaro in the form of faience object, which is a semi glassy material, (Sr. No. 1, Table II). This is a glazed siliceous ware, the body consisting of powdered quartz, moulded into shape as a powder held together by lime and soda, heated until the lime and soda have fused to hold the silica particles. It must be pointed out that the faience is not glass and the material is paleochroic. The chemical composition of this object is given in Table II, Sr. No. 1 [3].

Mesopotamian glasses

The earliest true glass of red colour is reported from the excavations at Ur. The specimen is red glass bead and is now stored in British Museum (No. 116582). No chemical analysis of this or contemporary specimen is available. However the earliest reference to the making of red glass using copper is found in the Mesopotamian Cuneiform glass texts of Tell' Umar. These have been very meticulously translated by Campbell and Gadd with the assistance of glass technologists[4]. These texts are dated to the seventeenth century B. C. These run into 43 lines. At present these are lodged in British Museum (No. 120960).

Chemical composition suggested for red glass

Among the chemical constituents to be added for making the red glass called as Santu (red) glass and Akkadian Santu (red) glass are lead, copper, lime and salt petre in varying proportions. The proportions have been rendered into modern notation by Harden[5] (from the above mentioned 1700 B. C. Cuneiform glass texts) e. g.

Glass	230	parts
Lead	40	,,
Copper	58	,,
Salt Petre	3·10	,,
Lime	5.0	,,

It is difficult to work out the exact composition of the first item e. g. glass; may be it was a vitreous material made of silica, soda, small amounts of alumina and iron, calcium and magnesium oxides. A very approximate composition of this could be 65%silica, 25% alkalies and 10% others and if this proportion is applied to Harden's figures the raw material for copper red glass of 1700 B. C. may be approximately :

Sand	45.0%
Alkalies	17.5%
R_2O_3+CaO etc.	7.0%
Lead compound	11.0%
Copper ,,	17 0%
Salt petre	1.00%
Lime	1.50%
Total :	100%

Genesis of copper red glass

The earliest use of copper compounds in silicate material to impart shades of red is met with chocolate coloured faience from Mohenjodaro; Sr. No. 1, Table II. After this innovation copper compounds were used to make red glass. Though the earliest red glass object of Mesopotamian origin e. g. the specimens from the Ur excavations, datable to circa 1800 B.C. have not been analysed, yet on the basis of the Cuneiform texts of 1700 B.C., we find the introduction of lead salt petre in red glasses, in addition to high and percentage of copper compounds for colouring red. From the chemical composition of glass of XVIII Dyansty Egypt from Tell el Amerna dated to 1400 B.C. (Sr. No. 1, Table 1); we find that the glass has low silica (51.85%), high alkalies (19%) and high percentage of Cu_20 (12.02%). Presence of 5.46% of $S0_3$ indicates the use of crude natron containing good percentage of Na_2S0_4. Later Egyptian glass of 2nd century B. C., (Sr. No. 2, Table 1) has much lower percentage of Cu_20 (2.5%). The presence of lead oxide (3%) and Mn0 (0.7%) are also notable.

Assyrian red glass of 8th-7th century B. C., (Sr. No. 4 Table 1) has high percentage of lead oxide (22.80%), Cu_2O (13.58%) and introduction of Sb_4O_6 (4. 07%), SnO_2 (0.32%) are noteworthy. The content of silica is low (39.50%). Broadly this glass has the composition of the Cuneiform tablet mentioned above. Roman Red glass, (Sr. No. 5, Table I) has the pattern of Egyptian glass of 2nd-1st century B. C. (Sr. No. 2, Table I); while glass from Pompli 1st cent. A. D., (Sr. No. 6, Table I) has broad resemblance with Assyrian glass. VIth century A. D. Byzantine glass has high percentage of SiO_2 (70.71%) low Cu_2O (1.26%). Small percentage of MnO is also present.

Chemical composition of Indian copper red glasses

Among the copper red glasses from Indian archaeological sites we find that specimens from Rajghat (Varanasi), Nalanda, Kausambi, Assam and Arikamedu e. g. Sr. Nos. 2, 5, 6, 7, and 8, Table II show complete absence of lead oxide. There is in general high content of iron e. g. Rajghat (9.67%) Nalanda (9.83+7.10= 16.83%), Assam (9.16%). The amount of copper or cuprous oxide is also high e. g. Rajghat (Cu_2O—5.27 %), Assam Cu-9.13%), Kausambi, (Cu_2O-10.89), Nalanda specimen has comparatively very low copper content (Cu_2O-0.49%), Arikamedu specimen has also low content of copper (Cu_2O -1.33%). Presence of 5% P_2O_3 in Arikamedu specimen is also noteworthy.

Taxila glasses, Sr. Nos. 3 & 4, Table II on the other hand are a class in themselves, these have low SiO_2 e. g. 37.09% and 39.79% in Sr. Nos. 3 and 4 respectively. Both of these samples have a high percentage of lead oxide e. g. 34.85 and 38.93 in Sr. Nos. 3 and 4 respectively. These compositions look to be inspired by the Assyrian influence (cf. the Assyrian composition e. g. Sr. No. 4, Table I,) .

Typical features of ancient red glasses

As seen from the account above, the ancient copper red glasses were generally opaque, probably opaque red was perferred on account of their similarity to jasper and coral. These have in general high content of cuprous oxide. In some cases elemental copper is reported, but it is uncertain as no specific test is mentioned for the estimation of metallic copper. The presence of lead in high proportion in red glasses looks to be purposeful and needs investigation by the modern glass technologists.

Modern red glasses colouring mechanism

Opaque red glasses are not a modern desideratum, transparent brilliant red glasses are required. As we have seen above that use of copper compounds to produce red colour in glass is of remote antiquity, yet due to exacting conditions required for production of red colour by use of copper compounds, copper ruby glasses are often not commercialised and the knowledge of the production

TABLE I

Showing the Results of Chemical Analyses of Glass Objects from Old World

Sr. No.	Details of the object	SiO_2 %	Al_2O_3 %	Fe_2O_3 %	MnO %	Cu_2O %	PbO %	Sb_4O_6 %	CaO %	MgO %	Na_2O %	K_2O %	SO_3 %	SnO_2 %	Total
1	1400 B. C. Egyptian xviii Dynasty Tell-el Amarna Haematinon Opaque	51.35	0.90	0.75	—	12.02	—	—	8.40	2.54	17.22	1.86	5.46	—	100.50
2.	2nd-1st cent. B. C. Egypt red glass	59.1	3.6	1.6	0.7	2.5	3.00	—	9.8	3.1	10.3	6.4	0.5	—	100.60
3.	2nd-Ist cent. B. C. Elephantine Egypt. Haematinon opaque.	58.45	5.00	0.86	0.53	2.09	1.28	—	10.69	3.42	9.02	7.55	1.37	—	101.26
4.	8th-7th cent. B.C. Assyrian Sealing wax red glass	39.50		4.35	—	13.58	22.80	4.07	4.40	—	9.71	1.91	—	0.32	100.64
5.	2nd cent. A. D. Roman Haematinon red glass	59.28	5.99	1.89	1.32	2.83	0.61	—	8.45	1.36	16.18	1.53	0.37	—	99.78
6.	1st. cent A. D. Pompii Haematinon red glass	49.90	1.20	2.10	—	11.03	15.51	—	7.20	0.87	11.54	—	0.65	—	100.00
7.	6th cent. A. D. Byzantine red opaque glass.	70.71	3.42	3.26	0.55	1.26	0.24	—	7.23	1.95	11.55	0.70	—	—	100.00

of such glasses was very limited and the mechanism of the colour production was not fully understood.

Exhaustive studies in the formation of copper red glasses by Atma Ram and S.N. Prasad [6] have cleared the controversies in this regard and conclusively proved that red colour in copper red glass is due to absorption of light by the particles of cuprous oxide of colloidal size disperesed in glass; rather than to the presence of metallic aggregates. However, when glasses are struck at higher temperature, the Cu_20 is mostly decomposed to metallic copper and small amount of undecomposed Cu_20 is sufficient to impart red colour.

The amount of copper or copper oxide required for copper red glasses has also been controversial, in old literature use of 15% Cu_20 is advocated; later work has shown that small amount of 0.1—0.2% Cu_20 was quite adequate.

Opacity, streakiness and heterogenity of cu-red glass might have been due to the excess of copper content.

Use of Nitre

Fuwa[7] suggested that the use of nitre intensifies the colour of the copper red glasses, this observation is of interest because the recipe for red glass of 1700 B.C. mentions the use of salt petre as an essential ingredient for red glasses.

Use of Lead Oxide

It is of interest to find that many ancient Cu-red glasses have lead oxide as a major cons-tituent. The purpose of this addition might be to reduce the melting point of the glass and also to improve the quality of the colour of the glass.

Observation of Vargin and Kozhin [8] that partial replacement af lime by red lead improves the quality of red colour, needs attention.

From the above account it can be said that glass technology of 1700 B.C. and even earlier had made significant contribution to the evolution of copper red glasses.

References and Notes on Tables of Chemical Analyses

[1] F. Neuburg, *Glass in Antiquity*, (English Translation), 1949, 3.

[2] M. G. Dikshit, *History of Indian Glass*, 1969, 5 et seq.

[3] P. Ray, *History of Chemistry in Ancient & Medieval India*, 1956, 15-18.

[4] C. J. Gadd and Campbell Thompson, A Middle-Babylonian Chemical Text, *Iraq*, III, 1936, 87-96.

[5] D. B. Harden in *History of Technology*, II, (Oxford), 1957, 316.

[6] Atma Ram and S. N. Prasad, Mechanism of Formation of Colour in Copper Red Glass, *Advances in Glass Technology*, 1962, (New York), 256—269.

[7] K. Fuwa, *Jl. Soc. Glass Tech.* 1925. 103 Abs.

[8] V. V. Vargin and N. P. Kozhin, *Jl. Am. Cer. Soc.*, 1934, 178 Abs.,

Table I.

Sr. No. 1—3. B. Neumann and G. Kotyga, *Z. f. angew, Chemie*, Vol. 38. 1925, quoted by. A Lucas, *Ancient Egyptian Materials and Industries*, 421.

4. W. E. S. Turner, *J. Soc. of Glass Tech.* 38., 445-66 analysis by H. J. Planderlieth, Brit. Mus. Lab.

5. B. Neumann, Antike Glaesser, II *Z. f. Angew Chemie*, Vol. 40, 1927, 964.

6. Bayer Pattenkofer, *Akad. Wiss*, 1857, 124. quoted by R. J, Forbes, in *Studies in Ancient Technology* Vol. V, 326.

7. Benrath Jakoby, *Sprechsaal*, 1884. 638. quoted by R. J. Forbes in *Studies in Ancient Technology*, Vol. V, 229.

Table II.

Sr. No. 1. P. Ray, *History of Chemistry in Ancient and Medieval India*, 1956, 15-18; Analysis by Sanaullah.

2. H. C. Bhardwaj, A Note on the Chemical Composition of Some Glass Beads from Rajghat, Varanasi *Puratattva*, Bull. Ind. Arch. Soc.), 1967-68; Vol. 1. 42-46.

3. Analysis by Sanaullah, A. S. I., A.R. 1921-22, 125.

4. and 7 analysis by Sanaullah A. S. I., A.R. 1922-23. 158.

5. and 8. Toranti, *Vetro*, IV, (1960), 23.

6. Sanaullah, A.S. I., A. R, 1930-34, 300.

Laboratory Studies in the Jokha Midden Soil Samples

by KARUNAKARA T. M. HEGDE

Jokha (20° 20′ N. 73° E.) is a small village in Kamrej Taluka of Surat District in Gujarat State. An archaeological mound here with the remnants of the Chalcolithic culture was first discovered by Professor R. N. Mehta in 1957 [1]. The mound is low, rising only two metres above the surrounding black cotton soil fields (Pl. IA).

In the field season of 1966-67 the mound was excavated by the Department of Archaeology and Ancient History of the M. S. University of Baroda. The excavation revealed six almost horizontal layers. In trench I, which can be taken as the representative of the other four, *mutatis mutandis*, the top two layers showed mixed materials belonging to the medieval and the early historic periods. This mixing was a result of deep ploughing of the surface of the mound with tractors. The four layers below were undisturbed. The layer 3 showed materials of the early historic period. The layers 4 and 5 revealed relics of the Chalcolithic period. The layer six was free from antiquities. The upper layers, one to four, were ashy and grey in colour. The layer 5 was fissured, clayey, compact and black. The layer 6 was silty sand, yellowish in colour.

Stratigraphy of Trench I at Jokha

Layer	Colour of the air dry samples according to the Munsell colour notation.	Period
1 & 2	2.5 y. 5/2	Medieval and Early Historic
3	2.5 y. 5/2	Early Historic
4	2.5 y. 5/4	Chalcolithic
5	2.5 y. 4/2	Chalcolithic ?
6	2.5 y. 6/4	Free from antiquities.

The Chalcolithic community at Jokha was essentially a microlithic one. But it supplemented its needs in implements with polished stone tools like chisels and celts and copper artifacts. The pottery predominantly consisted of plain and painted red ware and buff ware. On the basis of this pottery and the polished stone implements the Chalcolithic community is dated to *c.* 1500 B. C. [2].

From the outset, in this excavation, it was thought desirable to seek solutions to the five questions which the excavation raised. The questions were :

(1) What was the exact nature of association of the Chalcolithic culture with the black cotton soil ? (2) What environmental resources attracted the Chalcolithic community to settle down at Jokha ? (3) What was the source of potable water of the community ? (4) Why did the Chalcolithic community desert Jokha after being there probably for a considerable period of time ? (5) What was the relative density in occupation of the mound in the early historic period and the Chalcolithic period ?

During the excavation at Jokha, bulk of the Chalcolithic relics were recovered from the layer 4. But a part of this material was also recovered from the layer 5, which was, as noted above, fissured, clayey, compact and black. Almost all over western India, cental India and the Deccan, the Chalcolithic culture is intimately associated with the black cotton soil.

Writing editorially on the Chalcolithic culture in *Ancient India*, No. 12, Ghosh commented, *inter alia*, "Another feature of the culture is its general association with the black cotton soil. Except at Brahmagiri, where the soil is not encountered for the simple reason that the place is situated out side the zone of the soil and at Prakash, which is well within its zone but where the reason for its absence in the excavated area can only be a matter of speculation; the soil is present at all the centres. At Nasik, Jorwe, Tripuri, Bahal and Nevasa the respective excavators are definite that the relics of the culture were embedded well within the soil, at other places they are not certain about the inter mingling of the geological and the archaeological deposits. The question requires further examination", [3].

Since this comment, made a decade ago, a host of other Chalcolithic sites in association with the black cotton soil have been brought to light [4]. Therefore, an investigation to elucidate the reasons for intermingling of the archaeological and the geological deposits has been a desideratum. The excavation at Jokha gave us the opportunity.

In this connection, the following two questions are pertinent. (1) Whether the black soil at Jokha was fully mature when the earliest Chalcolithic community settled over the site ? (2) If the soil was mature, how did the intermingling of the Chalcolithic relics with the soil take place ?

Soil maturity is usually determined by a chemical analysis of the samples obtained from different horizons in a soil profile and establishing quantitatively eluviation and illuviation in certain soil constituents like iron, manganese, calcium, phosphate, humus and acidity in them. But such a study in samples collected from different horizons of the black compact layer 5 of the Jokha mound, would not be of much significance, as the chemical constituents of the layer could be expected to be modified by human habitation.

Therefore, mechanical analysis of the samples to establish grain-size distribution in them was carried out. Samples for this study were selected from positions close to the top of layer 5, free from the ashy seepage of the layer 4, but relatively rich in the Chalcolithic relics and also from the A_2–A_3 horizon of the undisturbed black cotton soil in Jokha from an area away from the mound and at present not subjected to agriculture. Samples of the midden soil for this and other analytical studies, discussed below, were obtained from the North and the East walls of Trench I, in the form of a column, approximately twenty centimetres apart as shown in Pl. II Representative results obtained by mechanical analysis through hydrometer method are given below (see also Fig. 1).

Grain-size distribution in the samples

Description of the sample.	Clay fraction %	Silt fraction %	Sand fraction %
Top of the layers 5 Trench I, East Wall depth 145 cms.	9.7	80.2	10.1
Top of the layer 5, Trench I, North wall, depth 144 cms.	9.8	80.2	10.0
A_2–A_3 horizon of the undisturbed black cotton soil near Jokha	10.5	79.4	10.1

The above table of results does not indicate appreciable difference between each sample.

Nevertheless, it is interesting to note the percentage of clay fraction in them as it is one of the indicators of the degree in weathering to form soil. The difference in the clay fraction in the black compact layer 5 of the mound and the undisturbed black cotton soil is very small which varies from 0.8 % to 0.7%. From this observation it is possible to indicate that the black soil at Jokha was almost as much mature as it is today, when the earliest Chalcolithic community settled over the site. How then, did the Chalcolithic relics intermingle with the black soil ?

The black soil at Jokha is an excellent loam, rich in clay and humus. A quantitative estimation of the alkali soluble humus fraction in the undisturbed soil samples and the samples from the layer 5 of the mound indicated 2.42% and 2.28% respectively. This fraction is roughly one third of the entire humus complex present in the soil.

A clayey deposit without humus expands when wet and shrinks when dry, giving rise to extreme sticky consistency in the monsoon season and wide fissures in the summer season. When a clayey deposit is a soil rich in humus,

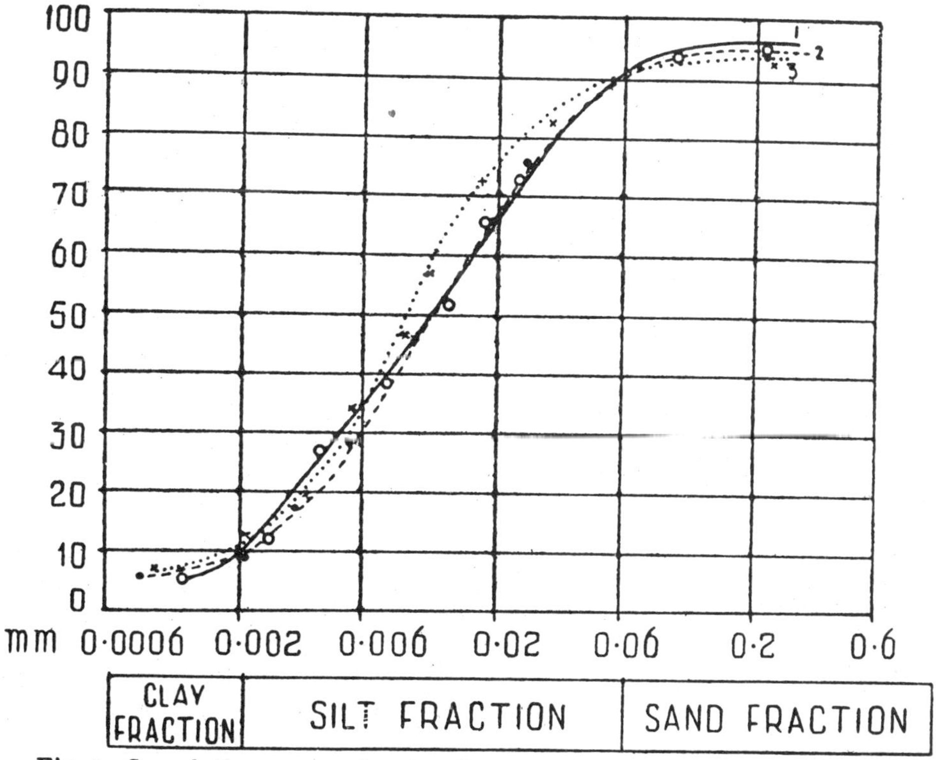

Fig. 1. Cumulative curves showing the grainsize distribution in the black soil within the archaeological mound and out side at Jokha. Curve 1 represents sample from top of L. 5, Tr. I, east wall at 145 cms. depth. Curve 2 represents sample from top of L. 5, Tr. I, north wall at 144 cms. depth. Curve 3 represents the sample from A_2— A_3 horizon of undisturbed black cotton soil at Jokha.

such alternate expansion and contraction processes in it become pronounced as humus itself swells when wet and shrinks when dry.

The combined effect of clay and humus in black cotton soil at Jokha is observed as frequent fissures in the soil in the summer season. Some of the fissures observed in the month of March, 1967 were more then 10 cms wide and a metre deep (Pl. IB.).

This annual fissuring in the black soil made it possible for the Chaleolithic relics penetrate deep into its interstices. The intermingling of the Chalcolithic relics and the black soil, therefore, is not due to contemporaneity in the formation of the soil and the habitation of the Chalcolithic community over it. On the other hand, the black soil at Jokha was almost as well formed as it is today, before the Chalcolithic settlement took place at the site. An extension of this study to the other Chalcolithic sites associated with the black cotton soil, may further support this observation.

The second and the third questions which the excavation raised, (1) why did the Chalcolithic community select this site to settle down and (2) what was the source of their potable water—are also equally intresting. Jokha is situated at least six kilometres away, as the crow flies, from the nearest perennial source of water, the river Tapi. There are no springs in or around Jokha. What then attracted the Chalcolithic community to this site ?

The black cotton soil at Jokha is over a metre thick. It is underlain by yellow silty sand. This silty sand deposit was formed during one of the river aggradation phases, probably in the late Pleistocene period. The thick black soil that caps the silty deposit is a result of weathering *in situ* of the former.

As noted above this is a loamy soil rich in clay and humus. It has low permiability and its moisture content is not prone to rapid evaporation. These qualities of the soil promote retention of moisture within the root zones of the cereal plants. In the course of the excavation at Jokha, saddle querns, well worn with deep circular depressions in the centre and pottery sherds with rice husk impressions were recovered from the Chalcolithic levels, indicating thereby that agriculture was one of the occupations of the Chalcolithic community.

On this soil, even scanty rain of 350 mms., if it is evenly distributed in the agricultural season, is capable of germinating the rice seeds and bringing them to satisfactory harvest. The mean annual rain fall during the last 20 years in Surat and its surrounding areas within a radius of 20 miles, which includes Jokha, has been 1058.4 mms. [5]. Therefore, it is possible to observe that the soil at Jokha held promise of rich agricultural harvest even during the Chalcolithic period. Studies in the animal bone remains recovered during the excavation from the Chalcolithic levels at Jokha indicate that hunting was one of the important occupations of the Chalcolithic people and the area held out promise of an abundance of game. Hunting and agriculture probably attracted the first Chalcolithic community to Jokha, situated on a wide fertile valley floor of black loamy soil. The first community may have settled on a natural eminance. What was their source of potable water ?

Though the land around Jokha looks like a flat rolling plain, a closer observation of the land surface reveals minor undulations in the topography. This has given rise to natural niches, where local accumulation of monsoon

A. General view of the jokha mound under cotton crop. Trench I in the foreground. Note the banana plantation in the background.

B. Jokha : Deep, wide annual fissures in the black cotton soil, phototraphed in March, 1967.

Jokha : A column of sample collected from the North Wall, Trench I.

runoff produces a pond. Such shallow ponds were probably the source of potable water for the Chalcolithic community. Five such shallow ponds, each containing several million litres of water were observed around the mound at Jokha in the month of March, 1967. There may have been many more during the Chalcolithic period as the land use under agriculture was limited.

Proximity of potable water and potentialities of agriculture and game notwithstanding, the Chalcolithic community at Jokha appears to have deserted the site after living there for a period of time. The excavation revealed that the occupation of the mound from the Chalcolithic to the early historic period was not continuous. Though, stratigraphically there was no discernible gap between the occurrence of the material remains of the two periods, the Chalcolithic potteries recovered from the upper horizons of the layer 4 were found to be weathered, rounded and their surface finish heavily deteriorated, indicating thereby that the material remains of the later Chalcolithic community were not immediately embedded, but exposed to the elements for some time owing to desertion of the site. What impelled the Chalcolithic community to move from Jokha ?

The excavation did not reveal any evidence either of fire or violence. There may have been an epidemic for which there was no evidence either. To help us find a plausible answer to this question, we obtained the meteorological data for Surat and its surroundings for the last 20 years from the Meteorological Department of the Government of India.

The mean rainfall during the last 20 years in this area has been 1058.4 mms. But the minimum rainfall within this period in 1948 was as low as 474.5 mms. Though the mean number of annual rainy days in the area in the last 20 years was 47.6, the low precipitation of 1948 was restricted to only 27 days. Further, closely following 1948, in consecutive three years of 1950, 1951 and 1952, the rain fall as well as the number of annual rainy days remained much below the respective mean values as given below :

Year	Rainfall in mms.	The number of annual rainy days
1948	474.5	27
1949	1147.3	50
1950	729.7	47
1951	605.5	34
1952	638.8	38
1953	1713.7	50

From the above table, it is possible to observe that such persistence in low precipitation lasting over three consecutive years would lead to draining away of the shallow ponds, which as indicated above, probably, served as sources of potable water to the Chalcolithic community. For want of water, the Chalcolithic community had no other alternative but to desert Jokha.

Today, however, a situation leading to desertion of Jokha for want of water is almost inconceivable. The entire area, including the archaeological mound is now subjected to intensive agriculture with round the year irrigation facility, drawn from the Tapi river, impounded nearly 90 kilometers upstream at Ukai. One of the irrigation canals known as the Katargam distributory main line, flows close to the mound on its northern side. This irrigation facility has vastly transformed the agricultural potential of the area, made the farmers already prosperous and secure within their homes.

But this intensive agricultural activity has also obliterated any subtle evidence that may have been there, within the mound, which may have enabled us to seek solution to the fifth question the excavation raised, namely, what was the relative density in occupation of the mound in the early historic period and the Chalcolithic period ? Quantitative estimation of phosphate and humus in samples collected from the layers 3 and 4 showed incomparable results. This was due to the use of both organic and phosphate manures on the mound and their penetration to the layer 3 through deep ploughing of the surface of the mound.

Acknowledgements :

Author's grateful thanks are due to : (1) The Director, Regional Meteorological Centre, Bombay-5 and (2) Professor R. N. Mehta, Head, Department of Archaeology and Ancient History, M. S. University of Baroda for encouragement.

Notes

[1] R. N. Mehta, *Proc. Ind. Hist. Cong.*, 1958, 210.

[2] R. N. Mehta, *et. al.*, *Jokha*, M. S. University Archaeology series No. 11, (under publication).

[3] A. Ghosh, *Ancient India*, No. 12, 1956, 2.

[4] H. D. Sankalia, *Prehistory and Protohistory in India and Pakistan*, Bombay, 1962, 152-225.

[5] Meteorological data for Surat and its surroundings supplied by the Director, Regional Meteorological Centre, Bombay-5, under his letter No. TE0/398 dated 7th June, 1967.

The Metal Technology of the Indian Protohistoric Cultures: Its Archaeological Implications*

by D. P. AGRAWAL

1. Introduction

In trying to reconstruct a past, which is essentially pre-literate, the immense role of technological studies cannot be over-emphasised. At times, even the shapes of corroded objects cannot be identified without using special techniques such as X—ray radiography [1].

In India, the period beyond ca. 400 B. C. is devoid of any decipherable records. Recent excavations, however, have provided ample evidence about the material traits of these protohistoric cultures. These artifacts or material traits when studied typologically do give important clues. But quite often morphological similarity may be deceptive; hence typological studies have to be supplemented by additional data on the technology employed. Below, we will discuss the salient features of the copper-bronze technology of the Pre-Harappa, the Harappa, the Copper-Hoards and the other Chalcolithic cultures†, and draw archaeological inferences from these data. In our discussions we will also take into account the ecologies in which these cultures thrived.

2. Technology

Metal technology mainly involves ore-extraction, alloying of the metal and metal-forging techniques. The distinctive techniques used can give us points of affinity as also differences amongst cultures, besides indicating the mines used.

We will discuss these processes under three categories : (i) Metal Forging Techniques; (ii) Alloying; and (iii) Ores used.

2. (i) Metal Forging Techniques

To determine the state of metal technology of a particular culture, the metal forging techniques used are a good index. We used metallographic examination as also surface examination of the artifacts for determining the original techniques employed. We will not expatiate on the techniques [2] here but give the results only.

The pre-Harappans were very poor in metal. The available evidence indicates that copper was being used on a small scale either because of lack of known local ores or due to the inability of the Pre-Harappan societies to afford full-time metallurgists.

The Harappans, on the other hand, show a sudden upsurge in metallurgical activity. They have a profusion and veriety of pots and pans indicating the knowledge of the techniques of 'sinking', 'raising', 'running on' etc. But no metal vessels are reported either from the Chalcolithic cultures, or the Copper Hoards. The Harappan and the Chalcolithic metal artifacts betray the knowledge of cold

---

* This paper summarises the results of an extensive study of the protohistoric metal technology undertaken by the author. [2].

† 'Chalcolithic cultures', in this article, includes mainly the Banas, the Malwa, and the Jorwe cultures.

working and annealing; but these techniques, surprisingly, were not probably known to the Copper Hoards people. Quite developed casting methods, including *cire-perdue*, were used by the Harappans. The Chalcolithic people seem to have used only open moulds. But the Copper Hoards show the use of close casting as indicated by the harpoons and the tell-tale ridges on some Gungeria axes. In metal forging technology the Harappans are most advanced, then come the Copper Hoards, and lastly the other Chalcolithic cultures.

In total metal inventory and abundance of metal, the Harappans lead the rest, followed by the Copper Hoards. The chalcolithic cultures are poorer in this comparison too; though far richer than the neolithic cultures of the south.

2. (ii) Alloying*

In west Asia, where metallurgy was mastered earlier than in India, occurrence of tin and nickel alloying was noticed in the I Dynasty grave goods at Ur [3] and from the Early Dynastic times [4] in northern Mesopotamia.

For pre-Harappa cultures the data are meagre. From Mundigak a low-tin (1.06%) bronze is reported [5]. The available analyses from Nal [6] indicate lead alloying only.

In the Harappan artifacts tin percentage greatly varies :

No. of Tools :	7%	10%	14%	6%
Tin Content :	1%	8%	8-12%	12%

These percentages are based on about 200 chemical analyses. Detailed tables and discussions have been published elsewhere.

From the data above it is clear that 70% of the Harappan tools were not alloyed and only 14% were alloved in the optimum range of 8-12% tin. The variations indicate that though the advantages of alloying were understood, yet correct proportions could not be controlled.

Tin bronze is more abundant (23% tools) in the upper levels of Mohenjodaro than in the lower levels (6%). Tin bronze was mainly used for making knives, axes and chisels. But the fact, that 70% tools were of pure copper only, indicates scarcity of tin.

In the Harappan artifacts arsenic alloying is also infrequent (8% tools); 4% tools only show nickel alloying and 6% artifacts lead alloying. It is likely that arsenic may have been used only as a deoxidiser for closed castings.

The Chalcolithic cultures have no artifacts alloyed with arsenic. Lead is common though and varies from 1–2%; it was probably a deliberate addition for better fusibility. As regards tin, a Jorwe axe has 1.78%; a Nevasa chisel has 2.7%; and the three Navdatoli specimens have it within 3–5%. It is obvious that tin alloying was known to these people, though it was not used in the optimum range of 8–12%. Tin, however, is significant by its absence in the Ahar artifacts.

---

* Pure copper is quite soft (89 Brinell Hardness) and very difficult to cast in closed moulds. It has atendency to 'gas' when cast, producing a porous casting. Addition of tin or arsenic considerably reduces this tendency as they function as deoxidising agents. Upto 16% tin and 4% arsenic form solid solutions with copper. Solid solutions have a greater hardness than any of the individual elements they are composed of, yet have sufficient ductility to be worked both hot and cold. If cold worked, the hardness is greater. For best results, the optimum range is 8-10% of tin. More than 1% of impurity in copper is considered as deliberate alloying.

Thus, we see that the high range of tin, lead and arsenic alloying of the Harappan artifacts stands apart from that of the Chalcolithic objects.

The evidence of alloying in the Copper Hoards is rather controversial. Smith [7] had mentioned four bronze samples from the Copper Hoards. This evidence is not so reliable, as most of these tools were taken from British museums and their exact provenance was not known.

Lal [8], however, found that the Bisauli anthropomorph contained 98.77% copper and 0.66% of nickel, and was thus unalloyed. The five Copper Hoard specimens* analysed by us too indicated absence of tin alloying. Thus the present evidence favours Lal's view that the Copper Hoards' people did not use alloying.

On the basis of the aforementioned evidence, we can thus tentatively infer that : (a) the Harappans were using deliberate arsenic, lead and tin alloying; (b) the Banasians were adding lead only; (c) the Malwa and Jorwe cultures were using lead and tin alloying only; and (d) the Copper Hoards were probably fabricated out of pure copper only.

2. (iii) Ore-correlations

The problems of ore- correlations are quite complicated. Desch [9] thought that nickel was the key element for identifying the mines exploited, which led him to the incredible origins of Transvaal mines for early copper in West Asia. Sanahullah [10] considered both nickel and arsenic as important for identification of the mines used. We will not go here into the inadequacies of these simplified approaches. For ore-correlations we have used comparison of the impurity patterns of the ore and the artifact, following Pittioni [11, 12], for determining the types of ores used we have calculated the probabilities on the basis of the statistical approach† given by Friedman et. al. [13]. It should be noted, however, that at the moment the data are not sufficient to warrant absolute conclusions; only tentative inferences can be drawn at this stage.

At Harappa and early levels of Mohenjodaro, the probability of the use of native or oxide ores is very high. Though on the whole, native or oxide ores were commonly used, yet use of sulphide ores on a limited scale is indicated right from the early levels. Use of oxide ore is further supported by the discovery of large quantities of such ore from a brick-lined pit in Room 51, D. K. area at Mohenjodaro [14]. Native copper and oxide minerals occur on the surface outcrops of ore bodies. The preponderance of the use of native and oxide minerals thus may indicate use of fresh mines.

The limited number of available analyses [15] of the Chalcolithic artifacts do not indicate any probability of the use of sulphide ores.

The analytical data for the artifacts of other cultures is too meagre to infer anything.

Tables 1 and 2 give the comparison of impurity patterns of the ores and the artifacts belonging to the Chalcolithic and the Harappa cultures respectively. It is important to note that Singhbhum pyrites showed absence of arsenic, antimony and lead, which are present in significant amounts in the Harappan artifacts.

* The specimens were : Shahabad celt; Shahabad harpoon (?); Kamdera. celt; Dhanbad celt and Dargoma celt.

† The details of technical data and the approach used have been given in a comprehensive book [2].

Table 1

Spectroscopic Analyses*

Key : +=present
nd=not detected
ns=not seen

Chalcolithic Sites

Sample Description	Ag	Fe	As	Sb	Pb	Bi	Cu	Sn	Ni	Zn	Mn	Co	Au	Al	Cr	Mo	Zr	W	Ti	Mg	V	Gd	P	Si
1. Navdatoli Axe	+	+	+	nd	+	+	+	+	+	+	+	+	nd	+	+	+	+	nd	+	nd	+	+	nd	nd
2. Navdatoli Chisel	nd	+	+	nd	+	+	+	+	+	+	+	+	nd	+	+	+	+	nd	+	nd	+	+	nd	nd
3. Chandoli Axe	nd	+	+	nd	+	+	+	nd	+	+	+	+	nd	+	+	+	+	+	+	+	+	+	nd	nd
4. Somnath Axe	nd	+	+	nd	+	+	+	+	+	+	+	+	nd	+	+	+	+	+	+	nd	nd	+	nd	nd
5. Ahar Axe	nd	+	+	+	+	+	+	nd	+	+	+	+	nd	+	+	+	+	nd	+	+	nd	+	+	+
6. Ahar Metal Sheet	nd	+	+	+	+	+	+	nd	+	+	+	+	nd	+	+	+	+	nd	+	+	nd	+	+	+
7. Khetri Ore	r.d	+	+	+	+	+	+	nd	+	+	+	+	nd	+	+	+	+	+	+	+	+	+	+	+
8. Nevasa Chisel 6721	+	+	+	ns	+	+	+	+	+	+	+	ns	ns	+	ns	ns	ns	ns	ns	+	ns	ns	ns	+
9. Nevasa Bangle 6722	+	+	ns	ns	+	+	+	+	+	+	+	ns	ns	+	ns	ns	ns	ns	ns	+	ns	ns	ns	+
10. Nevasa Bead 6723	ns	+	ns	ns	+	ns	+	+	ns	+	ns	ns	ns	ns	ns	ns	ns	ns	ns	+	ns	ns	ns	ns

* Nos. 1 to 7 based on [16] and 8 to 10 on [17].

Table 2

Spectroscopic Analyses*

Key : × = present
nd = not detected
ns = not seen

Indian Ores and Artifacts

Sample Description	Ag	Fe	As	Sb	Pb	Bi	Cu	Sn	Ni	Zn	Mn	Co	Au	Al	Cr	Mo	Zr	W	Ti	Mg	V	Gd	P	Si
TF-Cu-14a Madras Pyrrhotite	nd	×	nd	nd	nd	nd	×	nd	×	×	nd	×	ns	nd	nd	nd	nd	×	nd	nd	nd	ns	ns	nd
TF-Cu-14b Madras Pyrrhotite	nd	×	nd	nd	nd	nd	×	nd	×	×	nd	×	ns	nd	nd	nd	nd	×	nd	nd	nd	ns	ns	nd
TF-Cu-5 Mohenjodaro Galena Ore	nd	nd	nd	×	×	nd	nd	nd	nd	nd	nd	nd	ns	nd	nd	nd	nd	nd	nd	nd	nd	ns	ns	nd
TF-Cu-15 Singbhum Chalcopyrite	nd	×	nd	nd	nd	nd	×	nd	×	×	×	×	nd	×	nd	×	ns	ns	×	×	×	ns	ns	×
TF-Cu-24 Khetri Chalcopyrite	×	×	×	×	×	×	×	×	×	×	×	×	nd	×	×	×	ns	ns	×	×	×	ns	ns	×
TF-Cu-3 Chanhudaro celt	×	×	×	×	×	×	×	×	×	×	×	×	nd	×	×	×	ns	ns	×	×	×	ns	ns	ns
TF-Cu-6 Mohenjodaro spearhead	×	×	×	×	×	×	×	×	×	×	×	×	nd	×	×	×	ns	ns	×	×	×	ns	ns	ns

* My samples.

A closer comparison of the impurity patterns of the spectroscopic analyses (Table 2) of the Harappan artifacts and various ores shows that there is a close correspondence only with the Khetri ores. Singhbhum chalcopyrites and Madras pyrrhotite are quite dissimilar. The available evidence thus indicates that the Khetri belt is more probable a mining area for the the Harappans. This source alone can justify the Mesopotamian imports of copper from Meluhha [18] . A comparison of the spectroscopic impurity patterns of the Chalcolithic artifacts with the Khetri ore also shows a good correspondence (Table 1). At present, with the limited analyses available, we can only say that Rajasthan copper ores were probably used by both the Harappans and the Chalcolithic people. Geographical vicinity also supports such an origin.

3. Archaeological Implications

Let us first consider the typological evidence. The Harappans have very distinctive types : the razors; the arrowhead; the barbed fish hook and the curved blades. They even had the first true saw and the first tubular drills which show their ingenuity. The Copper Hoards are distinguished by the anthropomorph, the antennae sword and the harpoon—so well adapted for a hunting-nomadic life. The Harpoon was probably used for hunting big game [8] as also big fish. The antennae sword with its unwieldy (4" —5") antennae could never be used as a sword. The antennae could only be useful if they were used by fixing them, pointing upwards, on logs of wood in pits, and then big game could be driven into them. The anthropomorph with its heavy head and externally sharpened arms is obviously a missile. These points have been elaborated elsewhere [19]. The Chalcolithic cultures, however, have very simple types which are ubiquitous. The typology shows that at least the Harappa and the Copper Hoard cultures are distinct groups without any demonstrable affinities. The so-called 'links' have been shown [15] to be technologically much different than their alleged counterparts in these cultures. For example, in the Chandoli dagger the tang-end has been chisel-split and beaten back over the wooden (?) handle to prevent it from slipping and is technologically different from the 4" —5" long antennae of the Copper Hoards, which were cast as such. So also the Copper Hoards' anthropomorphs have invariably a distinct thickening on the head, whereas the so-called Lothal anthropomorph fragment is completely flat in section.

The Harappans came to an end around ca. 2000 B. C. at the metropolitan centres. The Chalcolithic cultures thrived from ca. 2000-1100 B. C. Therefore there is only a probability of the Banasians coming in contact with the Harappans. But the factors that go against any direct transmission of traditions and industries are many : (i) the part-contemporaneity of the Harappans north of the Aravallis and of the Chalcolithic cultures south of them; (ii) early pockets of apparently indigenous and unique cultures, e. g., the Kayatha Culture; (iii) largely independent areal distributions of the Harappans, the Chalcolithic cultures and the Copper Hoards and their temporal succession; (iv) in fact these cultures thrived in completely different types of ecologies; and (v) their significant differences in metal technology. The Copper Hoards most probably are post ca. 1200 B. C, and their technology also does not suggest [19] any interaction with the Harappans or the other Chalcolithic cultures.

Let us discuss further the ecologies, in which these cultures flourished.

The spatial extent of the Harappa culture coincides with a uniform ecological zone comprising semi-arid land, watered by perennial rivers, which provided vast tracts of fertile alluvium. The earliest civilisations of Mesopotamia and Egypt too had flourished in similar ecologies.

The Doab, on the other hand, was a completely different ecology. It was an area thickly wooded with monsoon fed forest and had kankry soil. These forest barriers effectively isolated the Copper Hoard culture from the western areas. This culture probably originated in the Chota Nagpur plateau which was rich in copper minerals and also in forests for fuel. The Copper Hoard's tool kit, especially the harpoon, the so-called anthropomorph and the antennae sword, is so well suited for a hunting-nomadic life. The forested Doab provided plenty of game and the river-fish. The Copper Hoard culture flourished in this distinct ecological zone and probably later in time than even the Chalcolithic cultures. Their metal technology as also typology of the tools shows complete isolation from the Harappans or the Chalcolithic cultures. If (at all) the Copper Hoards are not completely indigenous, they could only have a south-east Asian inspiration [19]. The prehistoric spread of Monkhmer dialects from south-east Asia to east India [20] and the suggested identification of 'Mundas' (linguistically affiliated with the Monkhmer) with the Copper Hoards [8]; the known neolithic contacts of east India with south-east Asia [21, 22] and now the Copper-Bronze age of Thailand going back to ca. 2300 B. C. [23]—all seem to make such an eastern inspiration probable, though conjectural at this stage [19].

The Chalcolithic cultures were confined mostly to the narrow alluvial strips, as they could not colonise the sticky black-cotton soil with their meagre copper tools. Thus the ecology severely limited their agriculture production; consequently, without the agricultural surplus, they could not come out of their village-status.

Thus we see that these main protohistoric cultures—the Harappa, the Chalcolithic and the Copper Hoards—thrived in different milieus, geographically separated, and largely at different times. Despite the evidence (e.g. the Black-and-Red Ware; the devolution of the Saurashtra Harappa culture) of some traditions having passed from the Harappan to the Chalcolithic cultures, the pre-ponderent evidence of time, space, ecology and metal-technology is against any direct cultural transmission. The present evidence thus indicates that essentially these three cultures were independent cultural phenomena.

Notes

[1] L. Biek, *Archaeology and Microscope*, (London), 1963.

[2] D. P. Agrawal, *The Copper Bronze Age in India*, (in Press), Munshiram Manoharlal, (Delhi).

[3] L. Aitchison, *A History of Metals*, Vol. 1, (London), 1960.

[4] V. G. Childe, *New Light on the Most Ancient East*, (New York), 1957.

[5] J. M. Casal, *Fouilles de Mundigak,* (Paris), 1961.

[6] H. Hargreaves, *Excavations in Baluchistan —1925,* (Calcutta), 1930.

[7] V. A. Smith, *Indian Antiquary,* XXXIV, 1905, 229.

[8] B. B. Lal, *Ancient India,* No. 7 1951, 20.

[9] B. A. A.S., *British Assoc. for the Advance of Sci.,* Reports for 1928-29, -30, -31, -33, -35, -36, -38.

[10] Sanahullah Khan in M. S. Vats, *Excavations at Harappa,* Vol. 1, (Delhi), 1950.

[11] R. Pittioni, *Archaeologia Austriaca,* Beiheft I, 1957.

[12] R. Pittioni. *Archeologia Austriaca,* Vol. XXVI, 1959, 67.

[13] A. M. Friedman, M. Conway, M. Kastner, J. Mflsted, D. Metta, P. R. Fields and E. Olsen, *Science,* 125, 1966, 1504.

[14] E. J. H. Mackay, *Further Excavations at Mohenjodaro,* Vols. 1 and 2, (Delhi), 1937-38.

[15] K. T. M. Hegde, *Jour. of the Orient. Inst. of Baroda,* XIV, No. 1, 1964, 84.

[16] K. T. M. Hegde,, Private Communication.

[17] H. D. Sankalia, S. B. Deo, and Z. D. Ansari, *From History to Prehistory at Nevasa,* (Poona), 1960.

[18] H. Levey, *Chemistry and Chemical Technology in Ancient Mesopotamia,* (Amsterdam), 1959.

[19] D. P. Agrawal, 'The Copper Hoards Problem.. A Technological Angle' (To be published in *Asian Perspectives,* IX, 1969).

[20] S. P. Gupta, *The Jour. of Bihar Res. Soc.,* 51 pt. 1-4, 1965, 1.

[21] A. H. Dani, *Prehistory and Protohistory of Eastern India,* 1960,

[22] J. Worman, *Science,* XXXI, 1949, 199.

[23] W. C. Solheim (II), *Science,* 157, 1967, 896.

A New Type of Neolithic Burial in Terdal, Mysore State

by A. SUNDARA

Background

Terdal, a big village of some historical importance in Taluk Jamkhandi, Dt. Bijapur, Mysore State, is on the Jamkhandi—Kudchi (a railway station on the Bangalore-Poona line of the South-Central Railway) road. Here is a Jaina temple [1] of some architectural interest with a dated (Saka 1044) inscription [2].

The village is situated at the foot of an extensive complex range of sandstone hills of the Kaladgi series covering a vast area on the east, south and southwest of the locality. In west and north, it is a plain land of the Deccan trap with very fertile black cotton soil. Thus, one, travelling from Kudchi to Jamkhandi, finds a sudden striking change of topography of the land from this locality onwards—from the plains of the black cotton soil to red hilly terrain. The hills are thinly wooded. About 3 km. north of the locality is the river Krishna flowing eastwards.

In 1944-45, A. M. Annigeri discovered some megalithic sites [3] in this and the nearby localities viz. Halingali, Hanagandi, Madalmatti and Asangi.

In 1964, in connection with my rasearch on megaliths in north Karnataka, I explored these sites for studying the megaliths there. Incidentally, I also examined an ancient site locally called 'Vibhūtimaḍḍi' in Terdal, mentioned in the *Gazetteer of the Bombay Presidency*, Vol. XXIV, Kolhapur, 1886, (p. 373) and found it to be a neolithic site. Subsequently I noticed three more neolithic sites [4] in this locality and about 21 sites in about 11 localities [5] west of Terdal and 13 in 11 localities [6] on the east, all in the valley of the river Krishna.

These sites yielded invariably highly lime encrusted animal bones, parallel sided blades, fluted cores occasionally with crested guiding ridge and microliths such as backed blades, crescentically retouched blades, single retouched points, crescents made on chert and chalcedony, thus technologically and typologically comparable to those of the chalcolithic Chandoli [7], Nevasa [8] etc., occasionally neoliths, especially axe of the pointed butt end type, and neolithic grey ware pottery of Maski fabric, in large quantities.

In many of the sites, particularly those west of Terdal, it is noteworthy that black-on-red painted pottery of the same fabric as that of the plain grey ware is more frequently found. It is comparable to that of chalcolithic Maski [9], Piklihal lower neolithic [10] and Brahmagiri IA [11].

Besides, in a few of these sites, there occurs another variety of plain and painted pottery analogous to that of Savalda [12] of the Tapi valley, in two fabrics viz., the red ware and the grey ware.

Further, remains of ash mounds, such as scoriaceous ash lumps, are scattered in about eight sites [13] including Terdal.

The megaliths of Terdal and the nearby localities are passage chamber tombs, not found in any of the other known site in the Deccan and south India and are thus unique. I have described these types elsewhere [14]. In view of their peculiar architectural features and geographical position, I selected some tombs of the types found in in Terdal-Halingali hill terraces and excavated them under the kind guidance of Dr. H. D.Sankalia in 1965-66.

Near one of the selected tombs in Terdal area, called Megalith I, was a round barrow of inconspicuous height (Fig. I). As is well known, round barrow unbound by circle of stones is one of the megalithic tomb types found in large numbers in the Deccan and south India and particularly in schist zone of Dt. Dharwar, the region under study. Many disturbed megaliths of this type in Dharwar Dt., have yielded pottery and fragmentary iron objects of the kind found in other excavated megalithic sites and burials in Sanganakallu [15], Brahmagiri [16] and Maski [17], during my explorations. Moreover, neolithic burials, excavated hitherto in India, do not have cairn packing of the magnitude usually found in the megalithic round barrows. Now, the round barrow in Terdal has many megalithic passage chamber tombs nearby on all the sides (Fig. I). In view of these facts, it was taken to be one of the megalithic types in the site and was therefore excavated. Contrary to the supposition, the excavation revealed that the burial was absolutely neolithic—containing articulated secondary skeletal remains of apparently one individual, four earthen vessels of neolithic grey ware of the kind found in the habitation sites of the locality, a copper bangle and a few microliths such as crescents and without megalithic pottery and iron—and not megalithic ! Further explorations, subseqently, led to the discovery of two more similar round barrows, one about 200 m. east of the excavated barrow in Terdal area and another about 100 m. further east of the second, in Halingali area (Fig. I, No-I in Terdal and No-I in Halingali). The barrow in Halingali was also excavated. But it actually did not contain either skeletal remains or burial furniture, but only a few stray sherds of the neolithic grey ware from the burial pit and of the megalithic fabric from the cairn packing. What follows is an account of the excavated neolithic burials of a new type by virtue of their having cairn packing like that of megalithic round barrows.

The neolithic burial, Terdal

The round barrow is situated about 2 km. east-north-east of Terdal in one of the terraces of the sandstone hills, in between 1925' and 1950' contours. Nearby this barrow are, on all sides, numerous megaliths of the passage chamber tomb types only. No round barrow other than the one in question, is found within a radius of about 200 m. (Plate I ; no. 1, 2. Fig. I). The known neolithic habitation site, Vibhūtimaḍḍi, is about 2 km. west of this and in the plain fields of the black cotton soil. Very faint traces of what may be owing to neolithic camp of very short period, are found near the eastern fringes of the tank of Terdal and about 1½ km. west-south-west of the round barrow. (Fig. 1).

The barrow, unbound by a circle, is roughly circular, 6 m. in diameter on average and about 10 to 12 cm. high at the centre, imperceptibly tailing off to the persent ground level. There was a tree grown in the middle of the barrow before excavation. It was cut off in order to get a clear view of the barrow for photograph. The barrow was excavated by quadrant method.

The cairn packing consisted of dark red earth and rubbles of sandstone, about 60 cm. deep at the centre and was immediately overlying a burial pit cut in the sandy red earth accumalated in a hollow of the sandstone rock. The earth of the pit was clayey and yellowish. The pit-line was, therefore, evident owing to the contrast of colours of the earth in and outside the pit.

The pit was ovaloid on plan: 1. 80 m. long, 40 to 60 cm. wide and 30 cm. deep and east-north-east by west-south-west oriented. It is slightly wider at the east-north-east end and is narrow at the other. The bottom of the pit is bed rock Fig. II.

In the pit are found human skeletal remains, four broken pots, a copper bangle, a parallel-sided flake and two crescents.

Human skeletal remains

The human skeletal remains, consisting of a few fragments of skull, front tooth of the lower jaw and two broken long bones, were fractional, laid in articulated and extended way along the longitudinal axis of the pit, on a 2 cm. thick bed of earth. The skull pieces were in the east-north-eastern part of the pit, while the long bones, near the other end (Plate IV A) These remains are being studied by Dr. K. G. Malhotra, Deccan College Post-Graduate & Research Institute, Poona.

Pottery

The pottery, crushed under the weight of the superimposing cairn, included a small pot with narrow neck and mouth, placed at the end of the long bones (Plate IV A, Fig 3) a bowl between the long bones and a similar pot and another similar pot between the upper end of the long bones and the skull pieces and on the left side of the lay out of the skeletal remains respectively. They are of neolithic grey ware of Maski fabric.

Copper bangle

The copper bangle (Plate III C; Fig 3 7) was rather appropriately kept inside the upper end of the right long bone, where wrist of the right hand would have been in extended positon. It had a green coating of cuppric oxide owing to rusting.

Microlith and parallel-sided blade

There were, in all, two crescents, a parallel-sided blade (Fig 3; 4, 5 and 6) and a bladish flake recovered from the earth of the pit. These were not found placed systematically like the other burial furniture such as pots. From the context of their occurrence, it is difficult to say that all were deliberately interred as burial furniture. At this juncture, it is worthy of note that flakes, fluted cores with well prepared striking platform, parallel-sided blades etc. are sparsely found here and there on these hill terraces. It is likely, therefore, that the microliths might have been there with the earth used for filling the pit.

One of the crescents was lying on the earth just overlying the pot, No. 3 and the other, found in the earth within a pot. The thick parallel-sided blade was found in the earth covering the long bones in between the pottery vessels 1 and 2 and about 2 cm. above the bones. And thick bladish flake of triangular shape occurred in the same part of the pit but about 8 cm. above the bones.

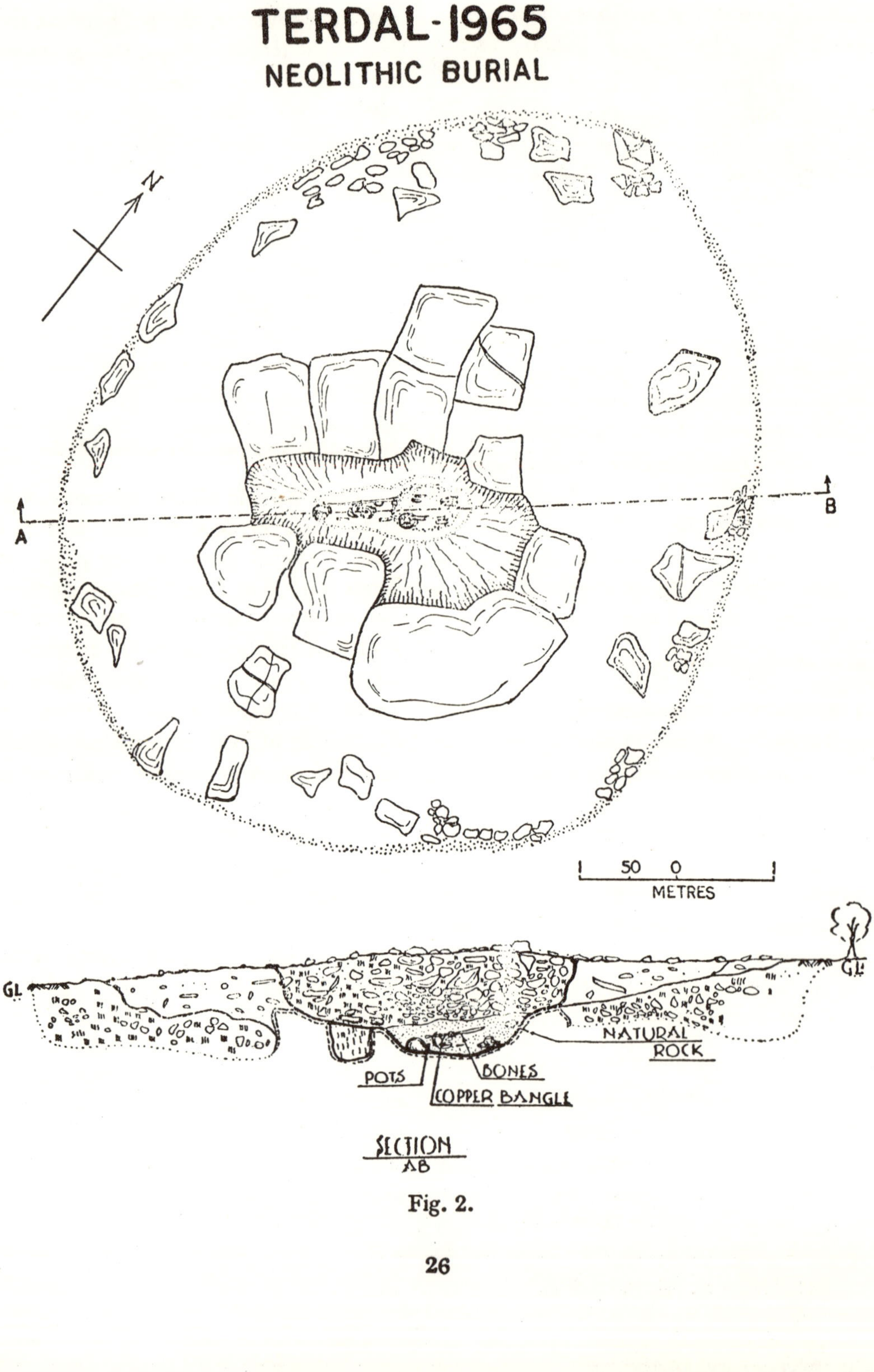
TERDAL-1965
NEOLITHIC BURIAL
N
A
B
50 0
METRES
GL
GL
NATURAL
ROCK
POTS
BONES
COPPER BANGLE
SECTION
AB

Fig. 2.

Objects from the cairn packing of the barrow

The earth and the stone rubble of the cairn packing yielded a few microliths and some megalithic potsherds.

The microliths were : a fluted core of chalcedony, four parallel-sided blades, two of them having retouch, three bladish flakes and six flakes and fragments, all of chert.

The potsherds were 31 in number—11 of black-and-red ware and 20 of red ware and were very fragmentary. There was no rim sherd in them.

The round barrow at Halingali

This barrow is also roughly circular, about 8 m. in diameter and about 15 cm. high from the ground level. It is about a km. west of Halingali, in a slightly elevated land of 1750 contour at the foot of the sandstone hill range. It is about 200 m. east of the above barrow. On its east, south and west are many magaliths of the passage tomb type (Fig 1, HGL No. 1).

One peculiar feature about this barrow is that there are three short round pillars, one each at the edge of it on the east, south and west.

It was also excavated by quadrant method. The cairn packing consisting of red earth and rubbles of quartzitic sandstone, about 60 cm. thick at the centre, was immediately overlying a pit, elliptical on plan and ronghly east-west oriented, situated almost in the centre of the barrow and equidistant from the pillars of the edge. The pit was 1. 80 m. long and 60 cm. wide in the middle and 40 cm. near the ends and 2 cm. deep. It was, unlike other burial pits, filled with stone rubbles and earth.

Neither skeletal remains nor burial furniture were found in the pit. However, at about 1 m. depth, four neolithic grey ware potsherds of Maski fabric including a small frgamentary out-turned featureless rim of probably a vase were obtained. Again from the south-east quadrant of the carin packing, at about 35 cm. depth, were obtained pieces of a fragmentary megalithic red ware pot.

Mere occurrence of a very few sherds of neolithic grey ware from the burial pit is not enough to take it to be a neolithic burial like the other one described above. Further, the presence of a crushed megalithic red ware pot at 35 cm. depth in the cairn packing is obviously in the first place not due to accident, but probably due to deliberate attempt [18] of interring a broken pot in connection with the burial ritual in the cairn packing some time after its erection. Thus, it does not indicate that the barrow is megalithic. However, since this type of megalithic burial is not found in the site, and if we take Terdal evidence into consideration, this round barrow also seems to be neolithic.

Some observations on the burials

1. The skeletal remains in the burial at Terdal are fractional, but articulated and extended and roughly east-west oriented. Obviously they are of one individual.

2. The pottery is entirely of neolithic grey ware of Maski fabric. Three of them have rounded bottom, globular body, very narrow neck and out-curling, flaring rim with featureless edge. Vessels, with extremely narrow neck of this type, are unusual in the neolithic levels of this region. Fragments of the crushed pot include pieces of two different [necks and rims suggesting that the vessel was double mouthed. The bowl has an external ledge on the body, a feature also uncommon in this type from the

other known sites of this region. A piece of a bowl of simialr type was picked up from Vibhūtimaḍḍi neolithic habitation site. The types, therefore, do not have exact parallels from the other sites [19].

4. The presence of copper bangle suggests the chalcolithic stage of the culture represented by the burial, which is otherwise neolithic.

5. Raising of cairn packing of large magnitude like that of the magalithic round barrow type is a unique feature known for the first time from this burial only.

6. The situation on the hill terraces considerably away from the habitation [20] is another peculiar feature of this burial.

Chronology

Raising of the cairn packing over the burial, a typical feature of megalithic burials, the presence of some fragments of megalithic pottery in the cairn packing and the location of the barrow in the midst of megalithic tombs, would apparently suggest that the burial was erected only after the arrival of the megalith builders [21]. Excavation of Megalith I in Terdal near the above burial (Fig. 1) yielded similar pottery. However, in view of the occurrence of the pottery of two different cultures, neolithic and megalithic, respectively from the burial pit and the cairn packing, it might also be possible that the cairn packing might have been added later on by the builder to the already existing burial.

Now, if the burial belonged to a phase when megalith-builders were erecting tombs as it would appear from the circumstantial evidences, it would then suggest either a phase of overlap or a survival of neolithic tradition in the megalithic phase. So far as the former is concerned, it is noteworthy that no megalithic habitation site has yet come to light here or in the surrounding areas, in spite of considerable intensive explorations. In none of the neolithic habitation sites in this and other localities nearby megalithic habitational remains are found. No indications of overlap of the two cultures by way of excavations in this part, for the moment, are available. Regarding the possibility of the survival of the neolithic tradition, it should be noted that while the builder of the neolithic burial could take over the laborious practice of raising enormous rubble packing over the burial from the megalith-builders, it becomes inexplicable the avoidance absolutely of the megalithic pottery and iron objects particularly when copper bangle could be afforded as burial furniture. Further, the pottery does not seem to include anything of the surviving phase. It seems that the megalithic potsherds got mixed with the cairn packing after the burial was erected. It may be mentioned that a few burrows were present in the cairn, which were caused by natural agencies, and this factor may account for the presence of megalthic potsherds in the cairn packing. However, if we rely upon this evidence, we are taking it for granted that the burial and cairn packing belong to one and the same period and the people of the succeding megalithic phase were in no way associated with the Contruction of the barrow under discussion.

The question of adding the cairn packing to the already existing burial is not borne out by the stratigrphay of the burial. There is no sterile layer of soil in between the cairn packing and the top of the undisturbed burial pit suggesting the gap of time.

From the above discussion, it is very likely that the round barrow was already there

A. Terdal : Neolithic round barrow with megaliths in the background.

B. Terdal : Neolithic round barrow ; close view.

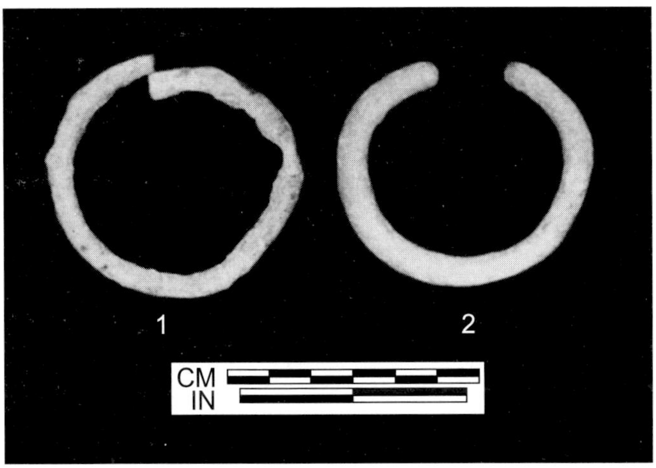

C. Terdal : Copper bangles:
1. from the vibutimaddi neolithic habitation-site;
2. from the neolithic burial.

A. Terdal : The Neolithic burial.

B. Sunet Sealing.

C. A Vaiṣṇava Sealing from Jhusi.

before the megalith builders arrived there. That the neolithic people were moving about in these hills is evident from the sparse presence of microliths, parallel-sided blades, fluted cores, flakes and fragments of chert and chalcedony and of the feeble traces of what appears to be camp site near the tank (Fig 1). And when erection of cairn over a burial is intended, naturally, owing to availability of required material for it in the hills, the hill terraces were preferred as burial site away from the habitation area. Probably this practice came into vogue at a later stage of the neolithic period on a small scale, which accounts for the extremely limited number of neolithic round barrows. If there were a few more burials at the foot of the hills, the surface indication of these must have been removed when the land was brought under cultivation.

In the light of the above analysis of the evidences, the round barrow may provisionally be ascribed to a phase immediately preceding the Iron Age megalithic phase, i. e., the late phase of the neolithic culture in the chalcolithic stage before the intrusion of the megalithic culture in this part.

The C—14 datings of the charcoal samples from the earliest two layers [22] of the neolithic habitation site (Vibhūtimaḍḍi) are : 2155±100 (2220±105), 3720±120 (1770 B.C.) and 3885±100 (1935 B. C.). A study of the antiquities from the surface of many neolithic sites of this part indicates that essentially the cultural characteristics are analogous to those of Piklihal lower neolithic and Brahmagiri IA. It appears therefore that the neolithic culture had ended perhaps a little earlier in this part than in Krishna-Tungabhadra valley where by about 1000—800 B.C. the culture was intruded by the Iron Age megalithic culture. The round barrow may, therefore, be placed somewhere in between 1100-1000 B.C.

If the cultural phase ascribed to the round barrow, as most probably indicated by the present evidences, is proved correct by further work, then here is an instance that provision of cairn packing of large magnitude that can be called literally megalithic goes back to the upper phase of the neolithic culture which becomes a common feature of megalithic tombs of the Iron Age. In other words the earliest megalithic tomb type is the round barrow surviving from the neolithic in this part of Karnatak.

DESCRIPTION OF PLATES AND FIGURES

Figure I.

Megalithic site in the sandstone hill terraces of Terdal, Halingali and Hanagandi villages. Note the situation of the exacavated neolithic barrows No—I in Halingali, in the midst of megalithic passage chambers and also the striking comparative rarity of round barrows.

Plate III

A. Terdal : Neolithic round barrow in the fore ground and megalithic passage chambers in the background indicated by two standing persons. Megalith I, is indicated by the farthest person. For the relative position of the barrow, see also Fig. 1.

B. Terdal : Close view of the round barrow after clearance of the tree grown on it, before excavation.

C. 1. A copper bangle from the surface of Vibhutimaddi neolithic habitation site stat.

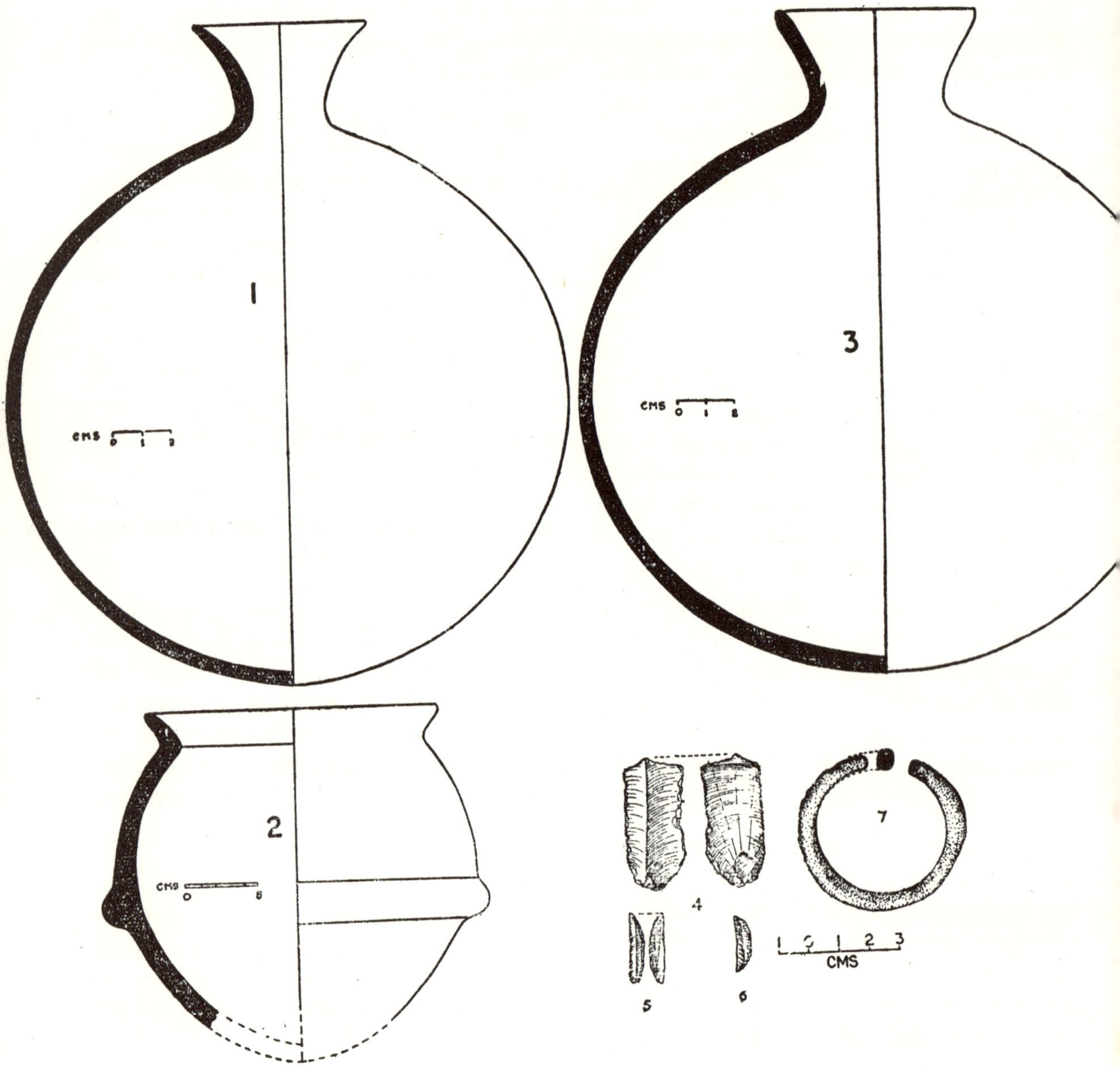

Fig. 3.

C. 2 & Fig 3. 7 : Copper bangle from the excavated barrow. The two ends of the solid copper wire, ovaloid in section, bent into a form of a bangle, are unconnected. It weighs 40 gms.

Plate IVA & Figure 2

The exposed burial at Terdel showing the human skeletal remains and the burial furniture (Nos 1 to 5).

Figure 3

Pottery from the barrow

No. 1. : A medium sized pot with round bottom, globular body, very narrow concave neck, and flaring rim with featureless edge ; of medium to thick section, rather coarse core and blotchy grey slipped externally and slightly burnished and micaceous.

No. 3. : Variant of No. 1. The body is somewhat squat, the neck, still narrower and thicker in section and the rim, slightly outcurling. Micacous dull grey slipped.

No. 2 : A deep bowl with round bottom slightly convex body with an external ledge and short out-turned rim ; medium to thick in section, blackish coarse core and blackish grey slipped.

Fragmentary small pot with squat body, narrow neck and out-turned flaring rim. It perhaps had another similar mouth on the body, like a spout. Of medium to fine core, unevenly thick section and buffish grey. Owing to some missing parts, it could not be reconstructed and illustrated.

Microliths from the burial

No. 4. Parallel-sided blade, thick and broad, of triangular section with slight retouch on the right edge of the ventral surface and chippings on both edges of the dorsal; of dark pinkish chert. Found in the earth about 2 cm above the long bones in between the pottery vessels 1 and 2.

No. 5 : Crescent of chalcedony, with slight retouch on the chord; found in the earth just overlying the pot 3.

No. 6 : Crescent of chalcedony. Found in the earth inside a pot.

Notes

[1] *Gazetteer of Bombay Presidency*, XXIV, Kolhapur, 1886, 374-5.

[2] Ibid.

[3] *Progress of Kannada Research Institute of Bombay State*, 1944-45, 23.

[4] A Sundara, "Protohistoric sites in Bijapur District", *Journ. of the Karnatak University Social Sciences*, IV, April 1968, 18.

[5] *Ibid*, VIII, nos. 94-104, 19,

[6] *Ibid*, IV, nos. 78-87. 18,

[7] S. B., Deo, et. al. *Chalcolithic Chandoli*, Poona, 1965, 33-46.

[8] H. D. Sankalia et. al. *From History to Prehistory at Nevasa*, 1954-55, (Poona), 114-149.

[9] B. K. Thapar, 'Maski : 1954 A Chalcolithic site of the southern Deccan, *Ancient India*, 13, 1957, p. 38.

[10] F. R : Allchin, *Piklihal Excavations*, Andhra Pradesh Archaeological Series, No. 1, (Hyderabad), 1960, 56-58.

[11] R. E. M. Wheeler, "Brahmagiri and Chandravalli : 1947 : Megalithic and other cultures in Chitaldrug District, Mysore State", *AI*, No. 4, 1947-48, 222-4.

[12] S. A. Sali : "A new ceramic of the Chalcolithic from Dhulia District, Maharastra State", *Journ. Asiatic, Soc. Bombay, 98*, 1964, 207-10, plate I; figs. 2-5.

[13] They are : 1. Bisnal; 2. Hippargi; 3. Kudchi; 4. Kullolli; 5. Sadalaga; 6. Saptasagara; 7. Shirguppi; 8. Terdal. Nos. 1 (Bilgi Taluk), 2, 4, 7 and 8 (all in Jamkhandi Taluk) are in the District Bijapur and Nos. 8, (Raibhag Taluk), 5 (Chikkodi Taluk) and 6 Athani Taluk), the District Belagaum.

[14] A Sundara, "Some new types of megalithic monuments near Terdal, Halingali, etc, Jamkhandi Tahsil Bijapur Dt. Mysore State", *Quarterly Journal af Mythic Society*, 57, (In press), Bangalore.

[15] B. Subba Rao, *Stone Age Cultures of Bellary*, (Poona), 1948, 11-13.

[16] Wheeler, *op. cit.* 209-20.

[17] *Op. cit* [9], 50-63.

[18] Such post-interments in the cairn-packing of the already existing magalithic burials are occasionally reported. In the excavations of a long barrow in Dec '66, by Shri S. R. Rao, Superintending Archaeologist, Archaeological Survey of India, South-Western Circle, Aurangabad (Dn), in the megalithic site discovered by me at Hunnur, Hukkeri Taluka, Belagaum District, Mysore State, small pot-burials were exposed in the cairn packing. I am extremely grateful to Shri S. R. Rao for his kind permission to refer to the excavations.

19] F. R. Allchin, *op. cit.*, 22-3. R.E. M. Wheeler *op. cit.* 202. Nagaraja Rao, *The Stone Age Hill-Dwellers of Tekkalakota*, 1965, (Poona), 27-33.

[20] During my explorations I noticed two neolithic burials; one exposed in the section of a well in Kullolli and another in the section of Bilgi-Bagalkota road-side cutting, very near Bilgi. It is particularly noteworthy that both are about 100 to 200 m. away from the periphery of the neolithic habitation sites located there. On the other hand, in the Krishna-Tungabhadra valley, the burials excavated so far at Brahmagiri, Piklihal, Tekkalakota, are right in the habitation sites. See the respective reports referred to above.

[21] Dr. Sankalia visited the site when I was excavating this and other burials there. We, including Shri M. S. Nagaraja Rao of Karnatak University, discussed about the probable phase of this burial. At the end of the excavations, Shri B. B. Lal, the present Director General, Archaeological Survey of India, also visited the site when I explained to him about the burial and showed him the antiquities. In 1967, I had discussed about this burial with Shri K. V. Soundara Rajan, Superintending Archaeologist, Archaeological Survey of India, Southern Circle, Madras, during his visit to Dharwar. I am extremely grateful to all these scholars for their kind suggestions and guidance.

[22] During the excavations at Terdal, I laid a small L shaped trench, 4m by 2m, in Vibhūtimaḍḍi neolithic site which had originally a mound of the habitational debris reduced now to the present ground level. In the excavations it was found that the earliest two layers were, undisturbed from which charcoal bits were collected for dating and sent to the C–14 laboratories of the Tata Institute of Fundamental Research, Bombay.

ACKNOWLEDGEMENTS

The excavations were carried out under the kind guidance of Dr. H. D. Sankalia, the then Joint-Director, Deccan College Post-Graduate & Research Institute, Poona and with financial aid of the Institute. I am therefore immensely grateful to Dr. Sankalia, and to the authorities of the Institute for their kind guidance, aid and permission for publication. The line-drawings of the burial and burial furniture were prepared respectively by Shri S. K. Joshi, Archaeological Survey of India, South-Western Circle, Bijapur, and Shri C. G. Padwal, Draughtsman, Deptt. of Archaeology, Deccan College Post-Graduate & Research Institute, Poona. The photographs of plate III were taken by Shri Krishna Potdar, Shrico, Commercial Artist, Dharwar, at my request. To all these friends I am extremely thankful for their fine work and ready and ungrudging help.

Daimabad—A Rediscovery

by M. K. DHAVALIKAR

Daimabad (Taluq Shrirampur, District Ahmednagar, Maharashtra) is situated on the left bank of Pravara, a tributary of the Godavari. The chalcolithic settlement at this place was discovered by Shri B. P. Bopardikar of the Archaeological Survey of India in 1958. Daimabad is a deserted village now and the name appears to have been derived from '*dālimb*' (in Marathi) meaning 'pomegranate' and consequently Daimabad, according to the local tradition, was once full of orchards of pomegranates. The ancient site is spread over an area of about 50 acres. The bund on the river near the site has actually protected it from the annual monsoonal floods but there is a great danger of the site being completely devastated by contractors digging for earth. In his recent visit to the site, the writer was pained to see that the trucks now regularly reach the site and that a large chunk of the southern part of the ancient mound has been dug out. This is going on incessantly in spite of the site being protected by the Government of India.

The ancient site at Daimabad is unique in several respects. The excavations by Shri M. N. Deshpande of the Archaeological Survey of India in 1959 have brouhgt to lighht several new features of the neolithic and chalcolithic cultures of Maharashtra which, even after ten years, have not been repeated elsewhere [1]. A careful study of the evidence from excavations throws important light on the beginning of the settled life in Maharashtra; its different phases of development and the evolution of the Jorwe culture. It is therefore proposed to analyse the evidence from excavations in which the writer had the good fortune to participate in 1959.

At the outset it is necessary to state briefly the culture sequence at Daimabad. The 20 feet thick cultural debris is divisible into three distinct cultural periods with appreciable overlap in between. The first inhabitants of Daimabad were the pioneering colonizers of Maharashtra. The cultural assemblage of this period has strong affinities with that of the neolithic farmers of the southern Deccan. The principal ceramics are coarse grey and red fabrics, frequently burnished; they are handmade and are sometimes painted with red ochre on rim. Besides, there are large handmade storage jars bearing incised and applique decorations. The occupation is also characterised by ground or polished stone tools, especially axes, and a specialised blade industry. Mention should also be made of perforated ring-stones. There is no evidence of the use of either copper or bronze during this period.

Nothing can be said about the houses of this period, for the excavation was confined to a very small area. They may perhaps be modest constructions with dwarf mud walls supporting wattle-and-daub screens. Patches of floor were noticed at places; they were made of rammed yellow silt. The dead appear to have been buried within the habitation area, but there is no clear evidence to show whether the burial took place within the courtyard or inside the house. Only one grave belonging to this phase was discovered; it was located within the habitation area. It was rather in a disturbed condition as it was partly cut by a later pit. No burial good was found accompanying the skeleton. But it is not unlikely that the burial furniture might have been destroyed by the later people who cut the pit into it. Moreover, it is also not possible to compare the burial with the funerary traditions elsewhere, particularly in the southern Deccan. Nevertheless the burial constitutes an important piece of evidence for it is the earliest of its kind in Maharashtra.

The earliest cultural phase does not seem to have last long, for very soon a group of people with different cultural traditions appears at the site. The overlap between the two occupational phases shows that both the groups of people lived amicably for some time. But the first farmers of Maharashtra were dominated within a short space of time by the new set of people who, from their cultural equipment, appear to have come from Malwa. This Malwa culture later becomes predominant. As Soundara Rajan observes, "everywhere we see two striking phenomena, that there is a basal matrix, affiliating in a differing degree, with a peninsular 'Neolithic' culture essentially of agro-pastoral type, and this is peacefully intruded into by copper using and painted pottery using culture groups of various categories ' [2]. But the stratigraphical evidence is nowhere clearer than at Daimabad.

There are no radio-carbon determinations available to us for building up a chronological framework for the Daimabad evidence. We have, therefore, solely to depend on the cultural affinities of the people with contemporary cultures. For the computation of the time-spread of the earliest cultural phase of Daimabad we have to take into consideration the problem of the two succeeding cultures, the Malwa and Jorwe respectively. The latter two, on the basis of evidence elsewhere in Maharashtra, can be said to have flourished between 1600—1000 B.C. The first cultural period of Daimabad is therefore pre-1600 B.C. The five-feet thick cultural debris of this period must have taken, as a reasonable guess, about two to three centuries to accumulate. The beginnings of the first period can therefore be placed in the opening centuries of the second millennium B.C. and we may therefore provide 1900-1600 B.C. as the time bracket for the first phase of occupation.

This dating is also supported by the archaeological evidence from the excavations. From their cultural equipment, these first farmers of Maharashtra appear to have come from the southern Deccan. A number of neolithic settlements have been discovered in the Krishna basin and the radio-active carbon determinations show that they can be dated to the end of the third and the beginning of the second millennium B.C. Very probably in the opening centuries of the second millennium these neolithic farmers started moving northwards in search of fresh pastures and new arable lands because of the pressure of a growing population; they possibly came through the Krishna and Bhima valleys to the Godavari-Pravara valleys. This, however, is the probable route of their migration and only further work in the Krishna and Bhima valleys can substantiate this hypothesis.

On the basis of the affinities between the cultural assemblages of the earliest inhabitants of Daimabad on the one hand and that of the southern neolithic on the other, Allchin has concluded that "this (Phase I of Daimabad) is close to the second or upper neolithic phase of the Karnatak sites to the south than the first phase" [3]. The upper or the secondary neolithic is datable in the later half of the second millennium B. C. and if we accept this dating, the Jorwe culture of Daimabad may well run into the first millennium B. C. The radio-carbon dates show that the Jorwe culture almost vanishes in the beginning of the first millennium. Moreover, the evidence from Karnatak sites shows that the upper neolithic is characterised by the use of copper, albeit on a restricted scale. It appears from the evidence of the black-on-red painted pottery akin to the Jorwe ware that they had already come into contact with Jorwe culture folk of the northern Deccan. In sharp contrast to this, the Daimabad evidence demonstrates that the neolithic people flourished here far earlier than the Jorwe culture folk and that they did not know copper. In fact, the evidence amply makes it clear that it should be equated with the primary of the lower neolithic of the southern Deccan. At the same time it is curious to note that the chronological chart of Allchin assigns 1800-1600 B. C. as the span for first phase of Daimabad which is quite near to that computed by us [4].

In the upper levels of the first phase of Daimabad, painted pottery of the Malwa fabric begins to occur in small quantities. This would only indicate the arrival of a new set of people, who, as their cultural assemblage shows, can be said to have come from central India. A huge painted jar of the Malwa ware constitutes an important find. However, it was not recovered from the stratified deposit but was found on the southern fringe of the ancient mound directly resting on the black cotton soil [5]. This has led the excavator to assign it to the earliest phase of occupation. It may, however, be stated in this connection that the earliest occupational layer resting over the black cotton soil has not yielded any Malwa pottery at least in the stratified trenches. The Malwa folk, who came to the site later, can be said to have settled on the black soil along the periphery of the mound. This was obviously due to the growth in population and the consequent enlargement of the habitation area. Be that as it may, the vase in question is a most beautiful piece testifying to the skill of the Malwa potter-artist. It is a globular jar with a beaded rim and is treated with a pinkish slip on the interior and with a thick buff slip on the exterior which is profusely painted with a jungle scene in two horizontal compartments. The upper compartment shows a muscular figure with two deer approaching it as if enchanted and peacocks in between; the lower has three tigers springing away in opposite direction. The human figure is solid while the bodies of the animals are hatched in broken lines. The whole scene has a telling effect and one feels as if the animals are paying obeisance to their lord, a sort of Paśupati of the later period. Exactly similar animals have been depicted on a vase fragment from Prakash (District Dhulia, Maharashtra) where it was found in Phase I–A [6]. "Such repertoire", according to Thapar, "must have been borrowed from the more ancient cultures in Iran although the present evidence is not sufficient enough to indicate the ancestry or inheritance" [7].

As already stated, there is an appreciable overlap between the first and the second cultural periods. Soon, however, we find the humble neolithic farmers being dominated by the Malwa people who can be said to have gained supremacy by virtue of their possessing superior weaponry. They had already mastered the technology of copper which they introduced in Maharashtra as the Daimabad evidence would show. Their painted pottery is also a distinct ceramic which is dressed with orange red or buff slip on which the painted ornament is executed in purplish to brown black pigment. Their tool outfit consisted of a specialized blade industry. However, the coarse red and grey wares of the earlier period continue to be used during this period as well.

The novel and unique feature of the Malwa culture that has been brought to light by the Daimabad excavation is the disposal of the dead. Only one burial belonging to this phase was discovered; it was a complete skeleton placed in a specially dug pit, in the north-south orientation [8]. It was, however, unaccompanied by any burial furniture. No burial of any kind has so far been reported from any of the Malwa culture sites in central India or elsewhere, and the Daimabad evidence, therefore, is the only of its kind. It thus represents an important feature of the Malwa culture which flourished in the northern Deccan. It may perhaps be a new trait which the Malwa people acquired in this region where the custom was already being practised by the earlier residents of Daimabad. It was therefore a result of the culture contact between the two people.

Another important feature of the Malwa culture which has come to light only by the Daimabad excavation, but has remained unnoticed so for, is the existence of spouted vessels in the Malwa ware [9]. Vessels with tubular spouts are conspicuously absent in the repertoire of the Malwa pottery forms; the only variety of spouts to be met with in this fabric is the characteristic channel spout. It is therefore needless to state that, in the light of the evidence from Daimabad the presence of tubular spouts in the Malwa ware becomes significant. These spouts are usually slightly curved and not straight as those in the Jorwe ware. It is of course difficult to visualize the form of the vessel from the spout. Fortunately there is only one fragment of a narrow mouthed bowl with a featureless rim which has been provided with a tubular spout [10] (Fig. 1–1). This spout, however, is straight. In all probability therefore the slightly curved tubular spout belonged to some other pottery forms. It is necessary to mention here that exactly similar spouts are to be seen in the neolithic pottery of the southern Deccan where they belong to jars with a flaring mouth and a blunt carination on the shoulder. Similar vessels are also present in the Malwa ware and these may perhaps have been provided with spouts. But it is difficult to be difinite on this point as there is no concrete evidence to substantiate it. It therefore seems likely that the Malwa people of Daimabad borrowed the idea of the tubular spout from their counterpart in the southern Deccan. These spouts appear to be handmade as their fabric would show; this also explains the bend in the middle. In sharp contrast to this, the tubular spouts of the Jorwe fabric are straight and were perhaps turned on wheel.

A solitary channel spout of the Malwa fabric has also been reported from Daimabad. This form of spout, however, cannot be said to be a characteristic feature of the Malwa

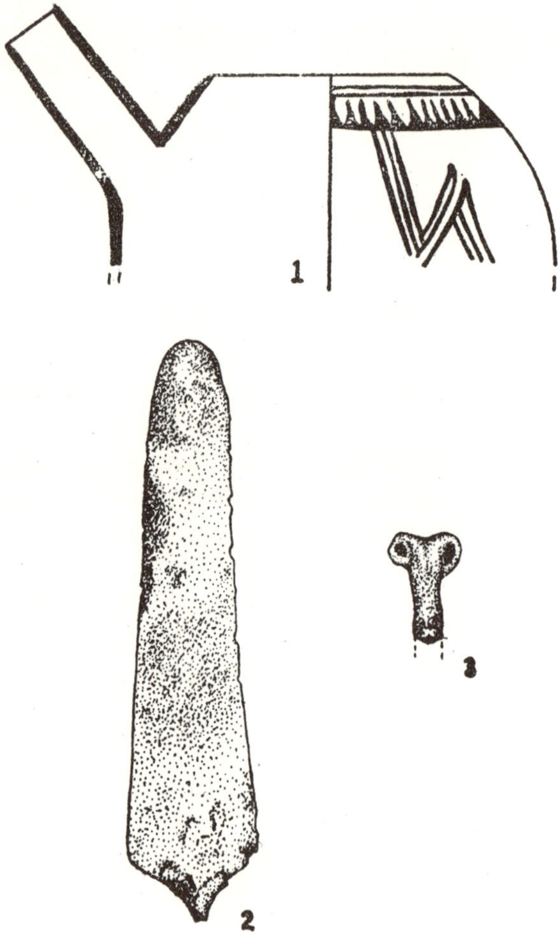

Fig. 1

ware for the simple reason that it is absent at a number of Malwa culture sites in central India and, even at Navda Toli, it begins to occur in the third cultural phase of its occupation. The idea of the channel spout thus appears at a later stage in the development of the Malwa culture. Although Sankalia's suggestion of its west Asiatic origin is plausible [11], it can nevertheless be stated that vessels with channel spouts are not uncommon at the neolithic sites of the southern Deccan. It is also significant that the channel spout in the Malwa ware should occur in Maharashtra where it is reported from Daimabad, Inamgaon, Prakash etc. It is also equally significant that not a single specimen of channel spout should have come to light in spite of three seasons work at Kayatha (District Ujjain, Madhya Pradesh), which is located in the heart of Malwa, not far from Navda Toli. At the same time it is noteworthy that channel spouted vessels in grey ware have been found at a number of sites in the southern Deccan where they are reported from the primary or the lower neolithic levels, the antiquity of which can be stretched as far back as 2300 B. C. [12]. In fact, a careful study of the pottery from such sites as Brahmagiri, Tekkalkotta, Piklihal, Sangankallu, T. Narsipur etc. shows that the channel spout probably evolved from the lipped bowl through the short channel. Even at Daimabad itself we have from the first phase a huge lipped bowl, approximating a short channel, in the coarse grey/red ware. It is decorated with applique designs of finger-tip indentations. The available evidence thus points to the borrowal of the channel spout by the Malwa people from the neolithic farmers of the southern Deccan. Perhaps that is why it occurs as late as phase III at Navda Toli which incidentally has also yielded some Jorwe ware.

It has already been stated above that the Malwa culture people introduced copper at the site. This is, in the main, evident from the fact that copper is totally absent in Period I whereas most of the copper objects that have been found in the excavations are from the second phase of its occupation. It is nevertheless clear enough that copper was extremely scarce. Among the repertoire of copper objects, especial mention should be made of two pieces viz., the knife and the pinhead [13]. Of the

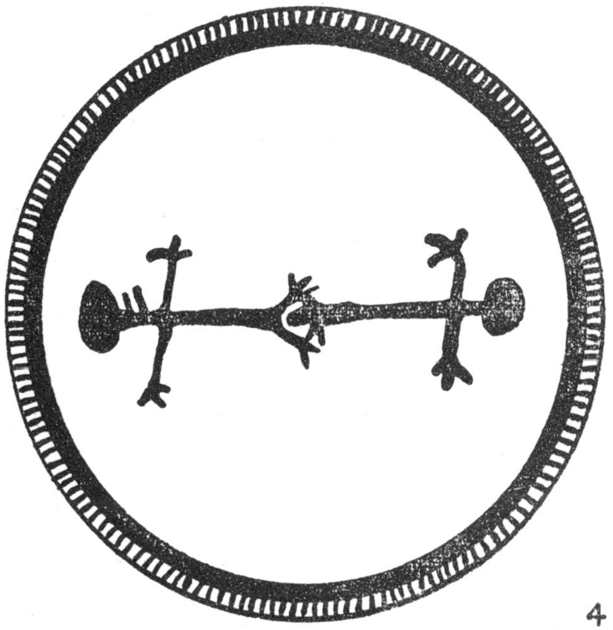

4

5

Fig. 2

two, the knife (Fig. 1–2) has more or less exact parallels at Harappan sites where such flat knives with handles have been found [14]. The parallel is significant and may not be without import. It represents yet one more Harappan element in the make up of the chalcolithic cultures of central India and the Deccan.

The pinhead (Fig. 1-3) is the only of its kind so far reported from chalcolithic sites in central India and the Deccan. This fragmentary specimen, on closer examination, appears to be a spiral headed pin which can be favourably compared with a similar one from the middle Harappan layers of Chanhu- Daro [15]. It is possibly a double spiral which, as Piggott has shown, is Iranian in origin [16].

Between the second and the third cultural phases of occupation again there is an appreciable overlap, and the new culture that emerges predominant is the well defined Jorwe culture with all its characteristic features. The red painted Jorwe ware is represented by such distinguished forms as the carinated bowl and the spouted *loṭā* in large numbers. A very interesting vessel of this period is a small bowl with an incurved rim, the interior of which is painted with two human figures, probably a male and a female, in sexual congress (Fig. 2–4). A very similar motif is painted on the interior of a pot from La Quercia in Apulia, a neolithic site in Italy [17] (Fig. 2.–5). The parallel is interesting and significant, but it is well-nigh impossible to say what it means in terms of cultural contact, for they are both far removed from each other in point of time and also space; at best it may represent the migration of the idea of a fertility motif.

The characteristic twin urn burials were found in good numbers. Besides, there was also a multiple urn burial consisting of three urns. They all contained the mortal remains of children while adults were interred in extended posture in a specially dug pit. Of the latter class a very curious burial was noticed in the middle levels of this phase. It was within the habitation area where, instead of digging the pit, the skeleton of an adult was simply placed on the ground. It was unaccompanied by any burial goods. The most noteworthy feature, that was noticed, was a series of postholes, found around the skeleton [18]. They have beeen taken to imply that a sort of canopy was erected over the dead, and the body has been supposed to have been lying in state before the burial. However, the ceremonious burial does not appear to have taken place probably because of some calamity that befell the family of the dead [19]. If the inference is correct, it can be said that the dead body was exposed to sun and rain for a certain period before the ceremonious burial.

A very important feature of the habitation of the Jorwe culture was a sort of embankment that was erected at the site with a view to protecting it from the river floods [20]. However, the excavation was circumscribed by time and resources and it is therefore difficult to know whether the construction was not a form of fortification which is more probable. Nevertheless it remains a unique feature of the Jorwe culture which has not been found at other sites so far. The building of such an embankment or fortification wall implies a tremendous community effort and the resources at command. We do not know whether it was meant for affording protection to the inhabitants from the onslaught of the iron age conquerors.

A most important contribution of the Daimabad excavations is that the evidence recovred is useful in tracing the origin of the Jorwe culture. This has become possible to some extent, by the threefold evidence of cultural sequence which has not so far been obtained from any other site. The coarse red and grey wares, which are associated with the Jorwe fabric, undoubtedly constitute a contribution of the southern neolithic farmers. The black-on-red painted pottery which is a distinguishing feature of the Jorwe culture has some characteristics in common with the painted ceramic of the Malwa fabric. It would rather be too superficial to observe that the tradition of painting in black over red surface is shared by both. But on closer examination it becomes apparent that there are many elements which are common to both. Thus the concave-sided carinated bowl can be taken to be derived from the bowl in the Malwa ware which is rather deep and has blunt carination [21]. Similarly the *loṭā* with a squat bulging body and high neck has a corresponding form in the Malwa ware [22]. The globular jar with a short or high neck is also paralleled in the Malwa chalcolithic [23].

The spouted vessel which is so characteristic of the Jorwe ware is, however, conspicuously absent in the Malwa ware. Spouted vessels, though rare in early Indian pottery, are to be met with in the southern neolithic pottery. In fact in the secondary neolithic of Brahmagiri, to quote (Sir) Mortimer Wheeler, "spouts are a familiar feature throughout the IB phase of the Brahmagiri stone axe culture" [24]. It is very tempting to compare T-46 of Brahmagiri, which is a *loṭā*-shaped vessel, with round bottom, out-curved rim and a slightly curved tubular spout [25]. But the nearest parallel, in form and function, is from Tekkalkotta, a neolithic site in the southern Deccan in the Krishna valley. It is reported from the earliest level, phase IA, representing the early neolithic strata assigned to the middle of 1800 B. C. on the basis of radio-active carbon determinations [26]. It seems most likely that the spouted vessel of the Jorwe ware is an imitation of its neolithic prototype. It, therefore, appears that the Jorwe culture was born out of the synthesis of the southern neolithic on the one hand and the Malwa chalcolithic on the other. The fusion of these two cultures took place most probably in the first half of second millennium and the locale, in all probability, was the Pravara-Godavari valleys, for it was only at Daimabad that we find all the three cultures.

The foregoing analysis of the evidence recovered from Daimabad excavations amply brings into relief the salient features of the site as also its importance which remained unnoticed so far. The site is of unique importance inasmuch as it has established for the first time a purely neolithic substratum in the prehistory of Maharashtra. It is needless to mention that the poineering colonizers of Maharashtra were the neolithic farmers from the southern Deccan who probably moved northwards from the Krishna valley to the Godavari basin through the Bhima valley probably because of the increasing pressure of population and in search of new arable lands and fresh pastures. They selected the Pravara-Godavari valley, which appears to have been endowed with a most favourable environment. The chalcolithic sites such as Daimabad, Nevasa and several others in the Pravara-Godavari valleys are located in a vast stretch of alluvium which is over three metres in thickness. This unusual accumulation of alluvium abuts against the steep scarp of the Ahmednagar plateau. This escarpment of the southern divide of the Pravara-Godavari does not appear to be erosional but seems to have had its origin in tectonic movements [27]. The rich alluvial stretch was probably characterised by thin vegetation and was well watered by the Godavari and its tributaries. It is therefore no wonder that the earliest farmers of Maharashtra were attracted by this most congenial environment.

The Malwa culture people arrived at the site sometime before the middle of the second millennium B. C. They appear to have got themselves naturalized in this region, so much so, that they adopted the novel custom of burying the dead. They also can be said to have borrowed the idea of the spout from their predecessors at Daimabad. This process of cultural fusion probably led to the birth of the Jorwe culture. All this would show that the ancient site at Daimabad is of great importance. It was only a season's work which has brought to light so many new features of the neolithic and the chalcolithic cultures that flourished in the Pravara-Godavari basin which incidentally was also the cradle of civilization of Maharashtra in the historic period. As already stated, the site is considerably extensive, and it can be said without any hesitation that, if excavated on a larger scale, it may yield evidence of crucial importance and throw light on the beginnings of settled life in Maharashtra.

Notes

[1] *Indian Archaeology : 1958-59-A Review*, 15-18. (Hereinafter this publication has been abbreviated as *IAR*)

[2] "The Devolution of the Peninsular Neolithic Culture–An Analysis of the Ceramic Influences", Paper submitted to the seminar on 'Pottery' at Patna, 1969 (unpublished).

[3] Bridget and Raymond Allchin, *The Birth of Indian Civilization*, (Harmondsworth), 1968, 192.

[4] *Ibid*, 196.

[5] *IAR 1958-59*, 16-17, Pl. XXII, B.

[6] "Prakash, 1955 : A Chalcolithic site in the Tapti Valley," *Ancient India*, No. 20-21, 1967, 48, Fig. 12, 3.

[7] *Ibid*, 35

[8] *IAR-1958 59*, 18, Pl. XXIV, A.

[9] The recent excavations conducted by the Deccan College, Poona at Inamgaon (District Poona, Maharashtra) have also yielded similar tubular spouts in the Malwa ware.

[10] *IAR-1958-59*, 10, Pl. XXIII, B.

[11] "New Light on the Indo-Iranian or Western Asian Relations between 1700-1200 B. C.", *Artibus Asiae*, XXVI, 1963, 314.

[12] For a discussion of channel spouts in the southern neolithic see I. Karthikeya Sarma, "Painted Pottery from Pusalpadu, Andhra Pradesh and further Explorations in the Cuddappah and Kurnool Districts", *Indica*, 4, 1967, 87.

[13] *IAR-1958-59*, Pl. XXI, B–2 & 3.

[14] E. J. H. Mackay, *Chanhu-Daro Excavations*, (New Haven, Conn.), 1943, Pl. LXIX, 2.

[15] *Ibid*, Pl. LXVIII, 9.

[16] Stuart Piggott, *Prehistoric India*, (London), 1962, 227. For an excellent illustration of a double spiral heaped pin see Mortimer Wheeler, *Indus Civilization and Beyond*, (London), 1966, 51-52, Fig. 73.

[17] O. G. S. Crawford, *Eye Goddess*, (London), 1957, 42, Fig. 11.

[18] *IAR-1958-59* Pl. XXIV, B.

[19] *Ibid.* 18.

[20] *Ibid.*

[21] H. D. Sankalia and others, *The Excavations at Maheshwar and Navda Toli 1952-53,* (Poona), 1968, Figs. 15-19, Types 19-21.

[22] *Ibid.* Fig. 42, Type 53.

[23] *Ibid.* Type 2.

[24] "Brahmagiri and Chandravalli, 1947: Megalithic and other Cultures in the Mysore State," *Ancient India,* No. 4, 1947-48, 224.

[25] *Ibid,* 228.

[26] M. S. Nagaraja Rao, *Stone Age Hill Dwellers of Tekkalkotta,* (Poona), 1965, 41, Fig. 17—A.

[27] G. Corvinus, S. N. Rajaguru & G. G. Mujumdar, "Some observations on the Pleistocene ecology of Western Maharashtra" (unpublished).

A Note on a Knot Design from Mohenjo-Daro and Its Occurrence in Later Times

by H. SARKAR & B. M. PANDE

A copper tablet having on one face an intertwined symbol (Fig. 1) and on the other an inscription, comprising four letters in the Harappan script, was discovered by Marshall at Mohenjo-daro. This unique tablet (no. VS 3526) came from Room 30, House 1, VS Area and belonged to the Late Periods [1]. Subsequently, another copper tablet (no. DK 3696) having an exactly similar symbol on one face was discovered by Mackay from DK Area, G. Section [2]. Both the tablets have a squarish outline, having almost similar dimensions. The latter, however, differs from the former example in that it has an additional line of three letters (or symbols) above the four-symbol inscription, which is common to both; the common line, according to Mackay, was an afterthought.

In the historical period, an almost identical symbol occurs on a "terracotta stamp with incuse devices" found in the Jandial temple at Taxila [3]. Ascribable to early Christian era, the stamp, about 2.37 inches in length, is made of brownish-red sandy-clay and has a conical handle. Needless to say, the device or symbol on the Taxila stamp is similar to the earlier two examples from Mohenjo-daro – the additional feature being a dot in each of the four knots and four dots in a vertical row in the centre, besides a borderline enclosing the motif

The same intertwined knot design appears to have gained some popularity in the Gujarat region during the rule of the Rāshṭrakūṭa kings. The following copper-plate grants from Gujarat contain the symbol, mostly along with the king's signature.

(i) The Kavi plates of Govinda (*Indian Antiquary*, V, 1876, 113). Here the symbol appears along with the royal signature. The inscription attests to the prevalence of Sun worship.

(ii) The Surat plate of Karkkarāja Suvarṇavarsha of Gujarat, dated Śaka 743 (*Epigraphia Indica*, XXI). Two such symbols occurring at the end of the inscription have been interpreted by the editor as *pāda-chinhas* symbolizing the foot-prints of Mahāvīra. The king, who was a staunch Śaiva, gifted a field to a Jain *vihāra*.

(iii) The Devali plates of Govinda, dated in the Valabhi year 500 (A. D. 818-19) (*Epigraphia Indica*, XXXV). It has been interpreted as *kolam* or *raṅgavalli* design still in vogue in south India.

(iv) The Prince of Wales Museum plates of Govindarāja, Śaka 732 (*Epigraphia Indica*, XXVI). The symbol is called here as an ornamental device after the royal signature.

(v) The copper-plate of Dhruva II, dated Śaka 806 (*Epigraphia Indica*, XXII). It has been interpreted as an ornamental symbol flanked by double *daṇḍas*.

(vi) The plates of Dantivarman of Gujarat, Śaka 789 (*Epigraphia Indica* VI).

KNOT DESIGN FROM MOHENJO-DARO

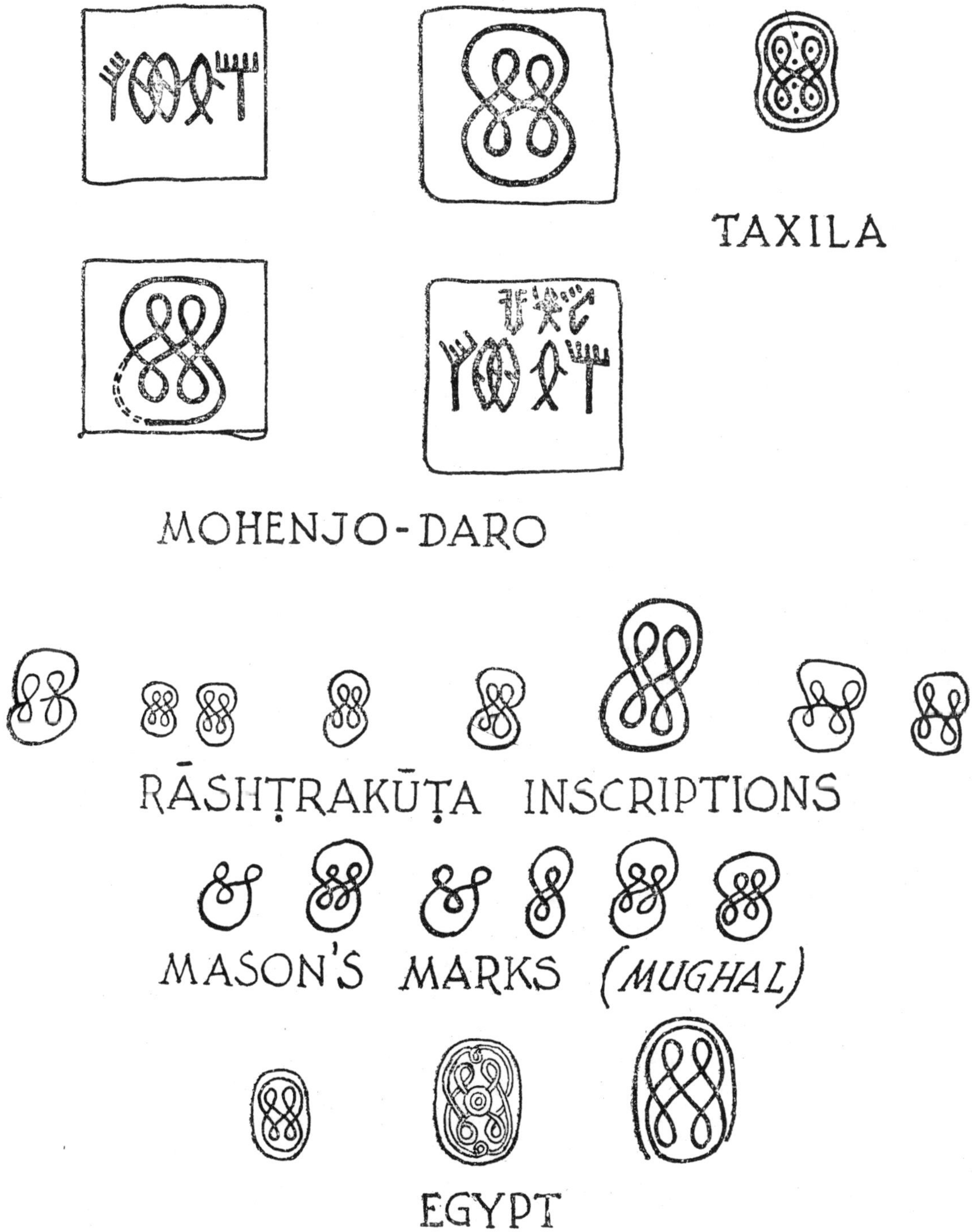

Fig. 1

The symbol occurs twice after the last line and a *śaṅkha*-design is incised below the first one.

All the copper-plates mentioned above are from the Gujarat area, and fall in the period between A.D. 810 and 884. It is worth noting that in all the examples the symbol occurs as part of the signature of the issuer of the grants. In the copper-plates of Govindarāja, Dhruva II and in the inscription from Kavi, it follows the donor's name, genera ly preceded by the expression *svahastoyam*. The detail in respect of the name of the scribe etc., is generally given after the signature and the symbol.

It is clear from the foregoing that the design, occurring for the first time on the copper tablets of the Harappan period, reappears in the historical and early medieval periods. That it did not go out of use after the early medieval times is evident from its occurrence as a mason's mark in the Mughal buildings at the Taj Mahal, Fatehpur Sikri and in the walls and buildings in the Allahabad Fort [4]. As a matter of fact, it survives till today as a favourite *raṅgavalli* motif in south India [5].

The evidence marshalled above will leave no doubt as to its sporadic character, for it has neither a historical continuity nor a uniform geographical distribution. Furthermore, at no period of its history in India, as its low incidence shows, the symbol attained any measure of popularity comparable to that of the *svastika*, spiral, or lotus. Of the Harappan sites, Mohenjo-daro alone has produced this particular type of knot design; in fact, the knot design itself is rare in the Harappa culture. Even the occurrence of the knot design, in general, in the Jhukar and the chalcolithic cultures of central India and the Deccan is not of much significance [6]. But particularly interesting is the fact that the knot design appears as graffito, for the first time, in the chalcolithic cultures of central India and the Deccan.

The endless knot pattern has a wide distribution in the areas of the 'fertile crescent'. An almost identical design is engraved on the scarabs dated between the thirteenth and the seventeenth Dynasties of Egypt [7]. According to Mackay, "very similar designs of looped and endless cord" are found on a pre-Dynastic jar of the Middle Period in Egypt. After citing a few more analogies, Mackay says that "though the pattern is not exactly the same as the one from Mohenjo-daro the resemblance is so close that these designs look to have had a common origin" [8].

It is not easy to find out the significance of this knot-and loop design which might have evolved from the magic of knots, so common not only in the primitive but also in some of the evolved cultures on the ancient world [9]. The endless cord, according to Mackay, is a symbol of longevity; whether the same significance was attached to it by the authors of the Mohenjo-daro copper tablets is difficult to say till the Harappan script is deciphered. The tablets, identified variously as seals, currency or amulets, conform to three regular sizes, viz., squarish, broad rectangular and narrow rectangular. Again, one of their faces contains, generally, an animal or a human figure or even a design or symbol, whereas the other face bears a legend in the Harappan characters. The uniformity in regard to size and depiction of the animals etc. (the animals invariably face right) points towards a certain amount of standardization; the extreme variation in weight, however, precludes the possibility of their being used as currency. That they were not used as seals is indicated by the low depth of incisions. Yet, the regularity in sizes, the recurrence of same devices with similar inscriptions, the use of permanent material like copper etc., may tend to show their use as family or guild tokens.

But the purpose of the copper tablets does not explain the significance of the knot device on the obverse. It may just be a magical or suspicious symbol adopted as guild-mark The use of knot design after the royal signature in the Rāshṭrakūṭa records of Gujarat might have had the same significance although here it may be identified as *pāśa* suggesting royal authority. However, whether the *pāśa* can be connected with royal authority is a question that needs explanation. It is well known that *pāśa* is an attribute of Varuṇa "the god who binds" and the lord of the western quarter [10]. His intimate connection with water also cannot escape one's notice as his *vāhana* swan or *makara* indicates. *Śaṅkha*, appearing with the knot design in the Rāshṭrakūṭa inscription, is also an attribute of Varuṇa, and suggests, at the same time, his connection with sea. In the *Ṛigveda* he is the guardian of truth as expressed by speech, and he is practically a moral god to whom prayers for forgiveness are offered by the hymnists. Thus, the use of this symbol after the royal signature carries behind it the authority and truthfulness, and both these aspects might have been connected with the knot-design on the copper tablets from Mohenjo-daro and tend to show their use as authenticated tokens in commercial transactions.

Notes

[1] Sir John Marshall, *Mohenjo-daro and the Indus Civilization*, (London), 1931, III, pl. CXVIII. no 5; described in Vol. II, 400.

[2] E. J. H. Mackay, *Further Excavations at Mohenjo-daro*. (Delhi , 1937, I, 364-65 and pl XCIII, no. 4 in Vol. II.

[3] Sir John Marshall, *Taxila*, (Cambridge), 1951, II, 437 and III, pl. 204 k.

[4] A. Gorham, *Indian Mason's Marks of the Moghul Dynasty*, (London), p. 9, nos. 40 and 41, p. 14, nos. 38-40 and p. 23, no. 71.

[5] *Raṅgavalli* is a term generally used in Maharashtra to signify the art of decoration by dry or wet pounded rice, sometimes even coloured, on the floor of the courtyard. In the north it is used on festive or ceremonial occasion, while in the south it is a daily ritual. In Hindi, it is called *rangoli*, in Tamil *kolam* and in Bengali *alpanā* (in the Kumaun hills it is known as *aipaṇa*). Every such motif has its name in the Tamil country and the endless cord designs have the suffix *muḍi* or knot. A device, very much similar to the peresent ones, has been called *Brahma-muḍi*. See, *Kalaikklanjiyam*, IV, (Madras), 1956, 329-33. *Brahma-muḍi*, according to the *Tamil Lexicon*, V, part I, 2687, published by the University of Madras, (Madras), 1932, is a knot of *darbha* grass (*kuśa*) used at a sacrifice.

[6] For Jhukar, see Ernest J. H. Mackay, *Chanhu-daro Excavations*, (New Haven), 1943, 142 and pl. L, nos. 4 and 4a. For graffiti, see B. B. Lal, "From Megalithic to Harappa: Tracing back the graffiti on pottery", *Ancient India*, No. 16, (New Delhi), 1960.

[7] Flinders Petrie, *Buttons and Design Scarabs*, British School of Archaeology in Egypt, Twenty-fourth year, 1918, XXXVIII, (London), 1925, pl. VIII, 128-130.

[8] Mackay, *op. cit.*, 364-365. According to him "it is to be found on beads of the etched carnelian type, both in Sumer and in the early Indus Valley, and is also known in early Cappadocia."

[9] For the symbolism of the knots, see Mircea Eliade, *Images and Symbols*, Studies in Religious Symbolism, (London), 1961, Chap. III–The "God who Binds" and the Symbolism of Knots, 92-124. Among the Indo-Europeans, the cords and knots have an importance for "the funerary divinities and the demons, and the magical use of 'binding' in popular medicine and sorcery". The symbol is also included as one of the Eight Glorious Emblems in Tibetan Lamaism and is considered as the "mystic diagram symbol of the endless cycle of rebirths." See, Antoinette K. Gordon, *The Iconography of Tibetan Lamaism*, (revised edition), (New York), 1967, 8-9.

[10] For the symbolism of Varuṇa *vis-a-vis* the knot see, Mircea Eliade, *op. cit.*, 95 ff.

Two Relic-Caskets from Mathura

by P. K. AGRAWALA

Through the kind courtesy of Dr. N. P. Joshi, Director of the State Museum, and his colleagues I recently had an opportunity to see and examine two relic-caskets of Mathura, now deposited in the State Museum, Lucknow. The two caskets, one of steatite and the other of crystal, in fact, represent a set of *dhātu-mañjūshās* as the latter (i.e. of crystal) was contained within the former (that is of steatite). For the two photographs (which show the lid of the steatite casket as detached and placed separately) accompanying the present note, we are thankful to Mr. O. P. Khaneja, Photographer, Department of Ancient Indian History, Culture and Archaeology, Banaras Hindu University.

Many such reliquaries and relics are known to have been found from the inside of a number of ancient Stūpas, mainly Buddhist, all over the country. For studying the attainments of minor arts and crafts in ancient India these precious and small antiquities provide a rich material that has been discovered from tims to time from excavations of Buddhistic edifices at Piprahwa [1], Sanchi [2], Bhattiprolu [3], Amaravati [4], Nagarjunakonda [5], Pitalkhora [6], Sopara [7], and many a other site [8].

In this light it seems likely that the two reliquaries described presently from Mathura were also discovered from an ancient Stūpa, and were employed for deposition of sacred relics or *dhātus* that were enshrined in the heart of that Stūpa. For the safe preservation of *Śarīra-dhātus*, together with some other pieces and tiny articles of ceremony, it had become customary to have a set of several reliquaries in varying shapes and sizes and also in different materials (such as crystal, gold, silver, steatite, other soft and hard stones, and pottery). The elaborate scheme and ingineous devices followed in the deposition of sanctified symbols and bodily relics in the heart of a Stūpa are amply known and explained more or less in their in tact and undisturbed preservation from the excavations that were carried out at Piprahwa, Bhattiprolu and Nagarjunakonda. The smallest of the caskets, which is usually a gold or crystal one, is found to contain sacred pieces and relics. It is, according to the practice or presumably some ritual, often found emboxed carefully in another casket, large enough comparatively to have inside it the first one. Thus in successive order according to the sizes the caskets are placed within one another, the largest receptacle being often in pottery.

Unfortunately we have no information recorded with respect to the contents, if any, of the two Mathura caskets (Pl. V A & B). A slip attached to them furnishes the following details regarding their place of discovery :—

Mus. No. 66·145 : discovered from the Chaubara Mound, Mathura. In the excavation of 1887–88.

From Cunningham's *Archaeological Survey Reports* (Vol. III, Calcutta, 1873), we are informed of a number of antiquities that were obtained from the Chaubara mound or mounds. Besides a small gold casket found in 1869 [9],

Cunningham during his work in 1871-72 found from mound A at Chaubara a steatite relic-casket of unusual shape exactly on the ground level in his excavation of a brick structure judged by him to represent a Buddhist Stūpa. [10] A line-drawing of this reliquary, in want of any other information aboubt it, is reproduced here (Fig. 1) from Cunningham's illustration of it.

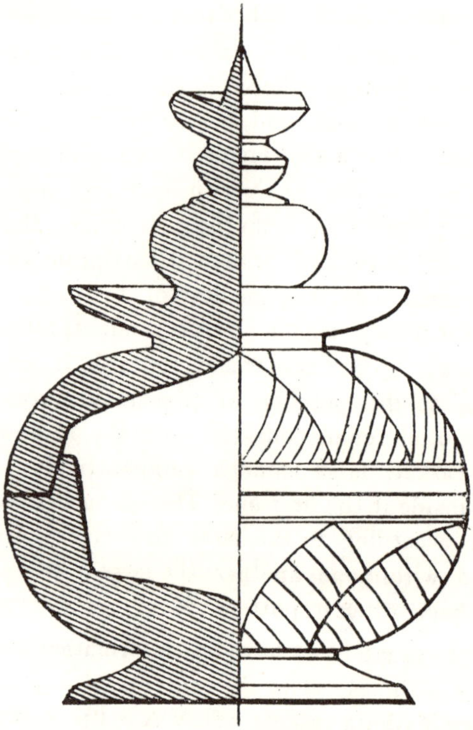

Fig. 1 Line-sketch of a steatite casket, found by Cunningham from Mound A, Chaubara.

Its comparison with the new steatite casket described below will be useful.

From the antiquities brought to light at the Chaubara mounds Cunningham concluded them to be Buddhist. (Cf. A large lion-capital now in the Indian Museum ; M 14 ; several fragments from a colossal Buddha statue.) [11] It is known that subsequent to Cunningham's work, Mr. Growse explored one of the Chaubara monnds, i. e. No. A, and discovered several antiquities of value that go to prove beyond doubt the existence of an ancient Stūpa on the site. [12] Some Kushāṇa pillars, railing cross-bars and rail-upright No. J 7 (Mathura Museum, showing Ṛishyaśṛiṅga figure on its one side and panels with scenes on the other) discovered by him from the same mound presumably belonged to the complex of a Kushāṇa Stūpa. An inscription (on a detached pedestal from some lost Buddha statue), dated in year 33 of Huvishka's reign shows that the Stūpa was in existence in the Kushāṇa period [13]. But Mr. Growse appears to have discovered no reliquaries from his digging at mound A, Chaubara [14], as he has mentioned nothing in this regard.

In shape the steatite casket is spheroidal and is made in two segments (as shown in the illustration placing them separately). The lower piece in its upper portion has a grooved section into which the other segment fits as the lid. Within it the smaller casket of crystal

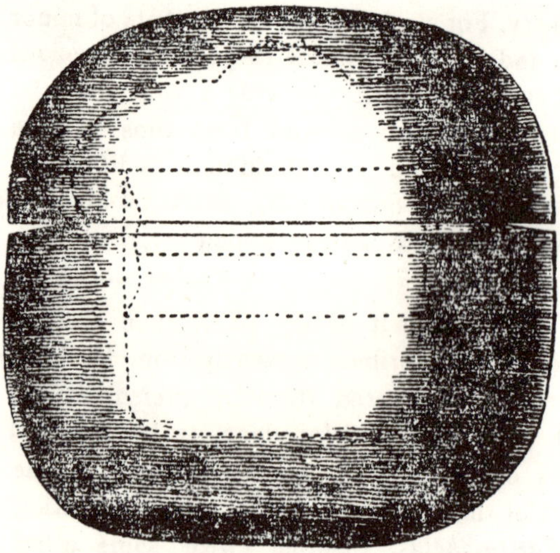

Fig. 2 Spheroidal stone casket from Bhaṭṭiprolu. After A. Rea.

A. Two relic - caskets from Mathura. In the State Museum, Lucknow. No. 66.145.

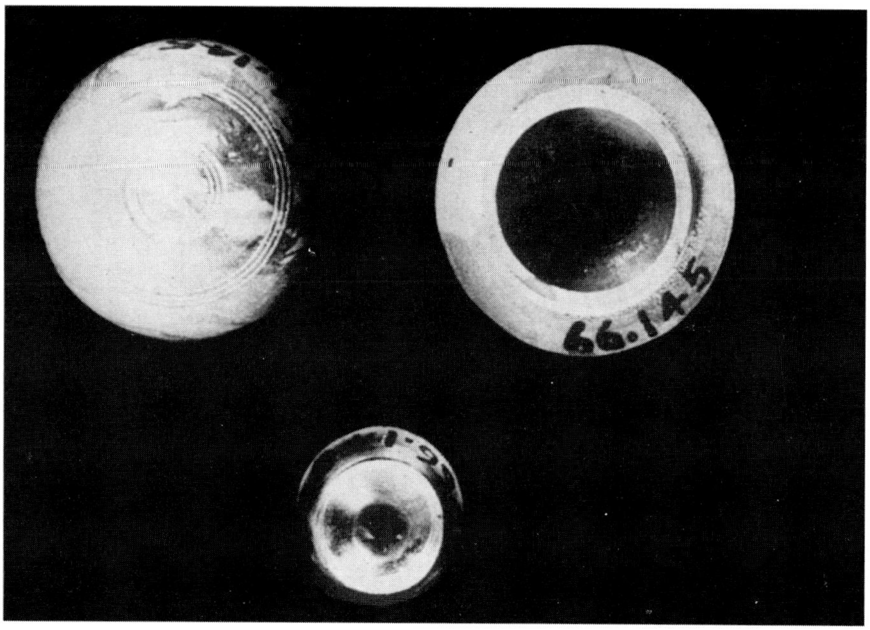

B. Same. View from the top.

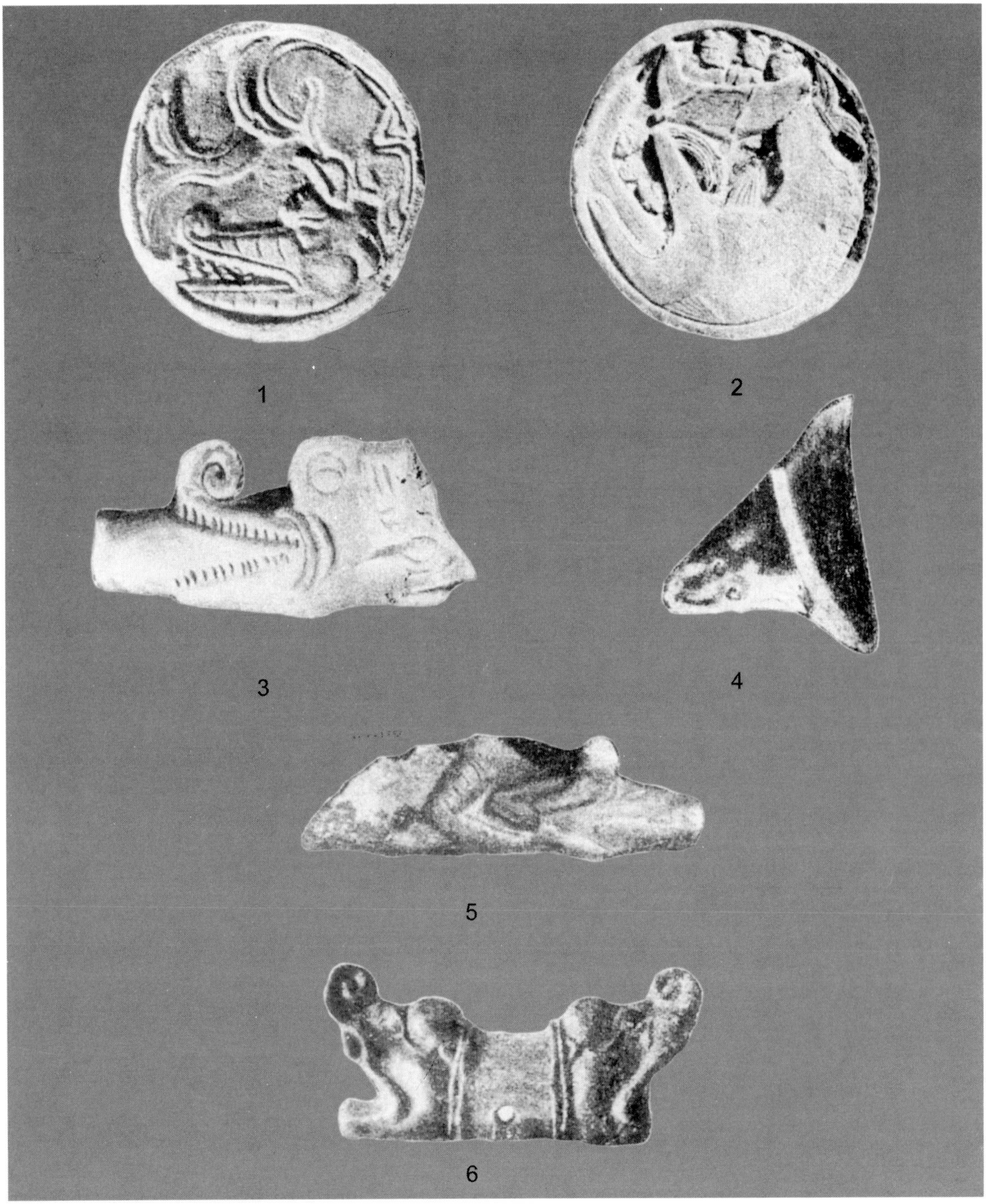

Makara -mukhas : 1. Kausambi, 2. Bharhut, 3. Rajghat, 4. Kumrahar, 5. Vaishali and 6. Nevasa.

was emboxed and it presumably had contained some minute pieces or sacred relic-bones in it. Here attention may be drawn to a somewhat similar globular stone casket discovered by A. Rea in his excavations of the Bhattiprolu Stūpa [15]. Besides the evident difference in size (and also in date), these two stone reliquaries, one from Mathura and the other from Bhattiprolu, may be said to represent a type which was inspired from a wooden prototype. Other seatite relic-caskets of similar type have also been found at Vaisali (from the heart of a Buddhist Stūpa; datable to B. C. 200) [16] and Taxila [17].

The inner reliquary of crystal represents a "phial"-shaped *Karaṇḍaka* with a lid. It is comparable in shape to a pottery *gaṛhā* of the present day ; with a difference with respect to its base which is flattened. A similar crystal casket has been recetly discovered from Amaravati, along with four others representing other shapes [18].

Both of the caskets are products of skilled workmanship and show remarkable finish with high polish. Keeping in view the date of other stone pieces and sculptures discovered from the Chaubara mounds, one can safely refer the two caskets to the Kushāṇa period. In the present state of our meagre studies of such minor pieces and antiquities, nothing as regards stylistic chronology and appreciation could be said.

Notes

[1] *JRAS.*, 1898, 572–588; *Sir Asutosh Mookerjee Silver Jubilee Volume*, III, 425-28; V. S. Agrawala, *Indian Art* (Varanasi), 1965, 82-3.

[2] A. Cunningham, *Bhilsa Topes* (London), 1854, p. 331; M. G. Dikshit, "Crystal Reliquaries in Madhya Pradesh", *J. of the Madhya Pradesh Itihas Parishad*, No.1 (Bhopal), 1969, 53-7, pl. II.

[3] A. Rea, *South Indian Buddhist Antiquities* (A. S. I., New Imperial Series, Vol. XV, Madras), 1894, 11 ff., pls. I, IV.

[4] *ASI-AR.*, 1909-10, 32; *Indian Archaeology 1958-9–a review*, pl. II A.

[5] Subramaniam, *Buddhist Remains in Andhra* (Madras), 1932, 22–3, pl. facing 22; *Indian Archaeology—a review 1958-59*. A. H. Longhurst, *The Buddhist Antiquities of Nagarjunakonda* (Delhi, MASI, 54), 1938, pl. XIII c, d, XVI.

[6] M. N. Deshpande, "The Rock-cut Caves of Pitalkhora", *Ancient India*, No. 15, pl. LXII B.

[7] Bhagwanlal Indraji, "Sopara and Padama", *JBBRAS.*, 1881-82, 307; K. N., Dikshit, "Buddhist Relics from Sopara re-examined", *J. of the Gujarat Research Society*, I, No. 4 (=*Dr. Bhagwanlal Indraji Commemoration Volume*; Bambay), 1939, 1-5, pl. facing 2.

[8] Moti Chandra, "The Art of cutting hard-stone ware in ancient and modern India", *J. of the Gujrat Research Society*, I, No. 71-85.; M.G. Dikhit, *op. cit.*

[9] A. Cunningham, *Arch. Sur. Report, for 1871-72* (Calcutta), 1873, 16. As noted by him at that time it was in the possession of Mr. F. S. Growse. Any other detail and the present whereabouts of this casket are not known.

[10] A. Cunningham, *op. cit.*, 17, pl. II.

[12] J. Ph. Vogel, *Catalogue of the Archaeological Museum at Mathura* (Allahabad), 1910, 13.

[13] H. Lüders, *Mathurā Inscriptions* (Göttingen), 1961, 54-55.

[14] If the time of discovery of the two caskets as known from the above mentioned slip attached to them, is taken to be reliable, the person who discovered them was, however, not Growse as he was transferred from Mathura early in 1877.—See Vogel, *op. cit.*, 8.

[15] Rea, *op. cit.*, 11-12, pl. I (below extreme left); line drawing 7 on pl. IV (being reproduced here as Fig. 2).

[16] *IAR., 1957-58*, 11, pl. IX b.

[17] John Marshall, *Taxila* (Cambridge), 1951, I, 327, III, pl. 80 C; dated on the evidence of a Karoshthi inscription of Azes (with year 134=A. D. 77).

[18] *IAR., 1958-59*, pl. II A.

A Vaishṇava Sealing from Jhusi

by KIRAN KUMAR THAPLYAL

A fragmentary sealing (Pl. IV C) from Jhusi (25°29′ North Lat. and 81°55′ East Long., near Allahabad) in the Allahabad Museum [1] shows in the upper field, from left to right, a *śrīvatsa*, a *gadā*, a *śaṅkha* and a *chakra*. The portion to the left of *śrīvatsa* is broken and missing. The preserved part of the legend in Gupta characters reads,

1...*Lokaikanāthasya*
2...*dyādikarttuḥ*
3...*rtasvāmino.*

The symbols are typically Vaishṇava. Śrīvatsa adorns the chest of Vishṇu. The *gadā*, *śaṅkha* and *chakra* may be identified as Vishṇu's *Kaumudī gadā*, *Pāñchajanya śaṇkha* and *Sudarśana chakra* respectivaly.

Lokaikanātha ('the sole lord of the Universe') undoubtedly refers to Vishṇu in the *Vishṇusahasranāma* [2]. Quite likely, *sarva* preceded the preserved part of the first line of the legend, and as such it was (*Sarva*)-*Lokaikanāthasya* ('the sole lord of the whole Universe').

The second line refers to the God as the first performer (*ādikarttuḥ*) of something which was mentioned in that part of the sealing which is missing. The third line we restore as (*ā*) *rtasvāmino* ('lord of the distressed'). But there would have been a few more letters preceding to it.

Jhusi has yielded a large number of Vaishṇava sealings. More than four hundred clay sealings [3] bearing variously typical Vaishṇava symbols like *śaṇkha*, *chakra* and *śrīvatsa* and the legend *Pannalābha*. The legend has been taken to be the Prakrit form of the Sanskrit *Paṇyalābha* [4], but may be a mistake for *Punnalābha* (=Sanskrit *Puṇyalābha* i. e. 'acquiring merit'). Further, more than two dozen sealings in the Allahabad Museum, from the same site, variously bear the legend *Padmanābha*, *Padmanābhasvāmin* and *Śrī Padmanābha*, and Vaishṇava devices like *śaṅkha*, *chakra*, *śrīvatsa* and lotus, singly or in groups [5]. In passing, it may also be suggested that seal No.88 in Marshall's list of Bhita seals [6] bearing the device of a *chakra* and the legend *Padmanābha* would have been brought to that site as *prasāda* from a Vaishṇava temple at Jhusi.

The sealing under discussion also seems to have been a votive offering to some such Vaishṇava shrine. The cumulative evidence of these sealings shows that Jhusi was an important Vaishṇava centre.

Acknowledgement

For facilities of study and permision to take photograph grateful acknowledgement is made by the author to the authorities of the Allahabad Museum.

Notes

1. No. 374
2. See also B. Ch. Chhabra, in *Indian History Congress, Proceedings*, 1954, 123.
3. This information I owe to Dr. S. C. Kala, Director, Municipal Museum, Allahabad. A large number of these are now in the Allahabad Museum.
4. B. Ch. Chhabra, in *Lalita Kala*, no. 9, 13.
5. E. g. nos. 299, 300, 368, 371, 247, 352, 353, 410, 344, 252, 335, 393, 246 etc.
6. *ASI, AR*, 1911-12, no. 88, 58.

Two Earth-works from Gujarat

by R. N. MEHTA

Introduction

Parts of Gujarat are lying in rather low rain-fall region in India. With its average rainfall of about 30″ per year, it is but natural that in the years of scarcity of rain-fall its population would suffer from the acute shortage of potable water. Moreover the erratic nature of the monsoon rain would lead to crop failure for want of a shower or two as could be experienced often.

In such a precarious condition, people in this region would be forced to take necessary precautions for conservation of the meagre fresh-water supplies. This is done by either tapping underground water through wells and step-wells or *Kuṇḍas* or by collecting rain water in small individual cisterns or large tanks or ponds. This activity must have left many traces of earth-works of different periods, as could be seen by the remains of large earth-works that were studied by the present writer in the Sabarkantha district and at Junagarh [1], Ghumali [2] and other sites.

The present work deals with two large earth-works. One of them is out of use due to breakage and the other is still in use.

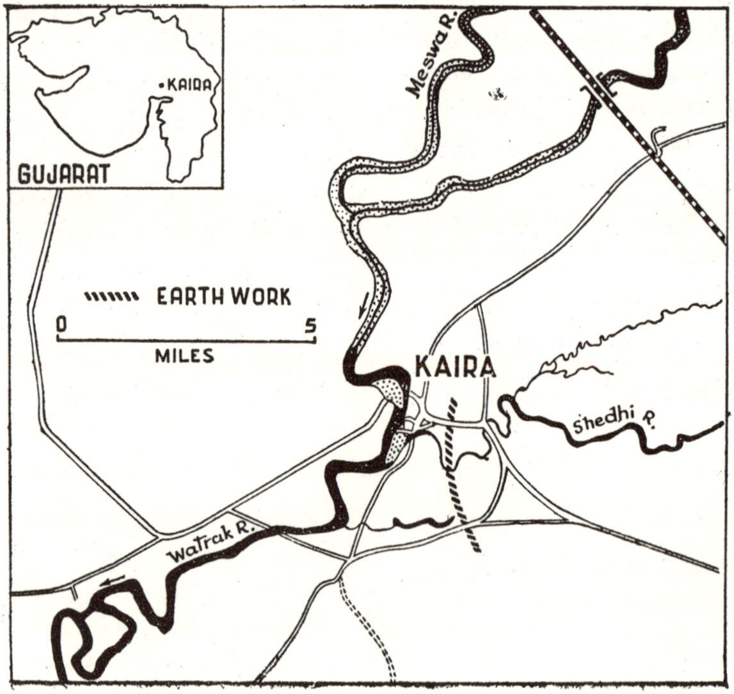

Fig. 1.

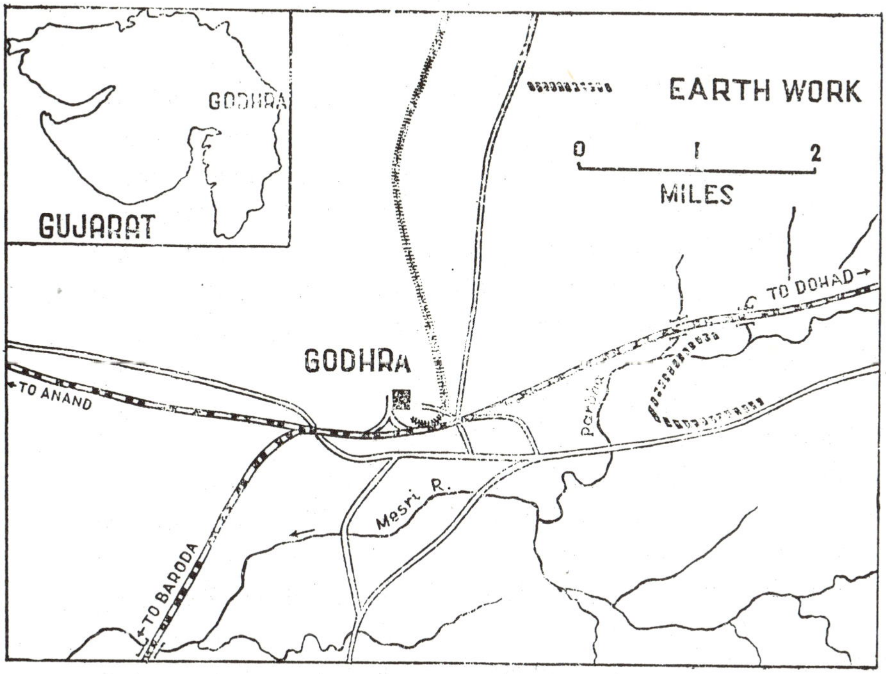

Fig. 2

Description of the Earth-work at Kaira

The first earth work (Fig. 1) that is described here exists near Kaira, ancient Khetaka, the headquarter of Khetaka Mandala.

To the south-east of Kaira, there is an earth work on which a Siva temple known as 'Paliya deva' exists. This is an 18 th century temple, but here a few Śiva liṅgas indicate that they are probably lower parts of rotary querns, which had their central axle also of the same material. Such an object was ideally suitable as a Śiva liṅga with its seat. This phenomenon was seen by the present writer at Gop and other sites, indicating the use of an older object in a new context.

The earth work on which this temple exists runs in a general north-south direction. It is cut by the national high way No. 8 running between Baroda and Ahmedabad. The earth-work runs in the south, towards the river Shedhi. It is washed away near this river but it continues on the south of the river Shedhi and runs for about a mile and a half before it disappears completely in the area under the jurisdiction of Vadsar village.

The earth-work is constructed of the yellow *Kankari* earth (Fig. 1). In a few cuttings some patches of black earth are also seen, indicating that the workers used the available material. The earth work is about 30 metres broad, 7 metres high at many places and at the top it is about 3 metres broad. This rhomboidal section of the earth-work and the arrangement of earth in the sections indicate that it is an artificial construction.

Today it is broken at some points, and is overgrown in many places by trees like *Babul*, *Neem*, *Sami*, *Piludi* etc. Many of them are large trees, which might be considerably old.

Chronology

At Kaira the tradition of this earth-work does not exist. People know this earth-work, but they do not throw any light on its history. This being the case, only archaeological evidence is adduced for chronology.

The evidence of 'Paliya-deva' indicates that the earth-work is earlier than the 18th century A. D., but a closer inspection of the bricks revealed some fragments with the breadth of about 10. 5" and thickness of 2.5".

A little to the west of this earth-work, a Śiva temple of mediaeval period exists. Here bricks of about 15″×9″×2.5″ were seen. They indicated the presence of some structure of the bricks of this size. The absence of tradition for the existence of this earth-work and the large size of bricks that are found on the earth-work indicate that it might have been made at least before the mediaeval period, possibly during the time when bricks of the size that are seen here were in general use. The evidence therefore seems to indicate that this earth-work is more than a thousand years old. It was possibly constructed during the period of the Maitrakas and Rāshṭrakūṭas when Khetaka was a place of importance

Purpose of the Earth-Work

The geographical position of this earth-work indicates that it might have been used as a dam to stop the flow of Shedhi and convert the area east of the dam into an artificial lake. Such earth-works of shallow streams are quite well-known in Gujarat as could be noted by the study of these in Sabarkantha [3], Girnar [4], Ghumali [5], and other sites, as well as the existing bunds at Godhra [6], Champaner [7] and other sites.

Description of Earth-work at Godhra (Fig. 2)

If the earth-work at Kaira is lying unused that at Godhra, that is noted here, is in use. It is the earth-work known as Kaneval. It is a long earth-work with partial use of stones and bricks. Its broader parts are 29 metres at the base, its height is about 5.5 metres and the breadth at the top is about 6.00 metres. The whole earth work is about 3 km.long.

This earth-work is in the form of a large semi-circle and hence seems to confirm the definition of a Sara as given in the Aparajita-priccha [8].

Chronology

A pumping station stands on a ruined temple belonging to the Chalukya period. Its lower plinth with parts of Bhita and Kalaśa are existing. It indicates that it was large and must have been destroyed at a fairly early date. After this, it seems that the general level of the earth-work was raised and over it another temple was built. Its foundation and parts of the stone structures are existing, but the upper structure has fallen down. This is a simple temple, probably of about 13th/15th century A. D.

These two evidences could easily indicate that this earth-work must belong to the Chālukayan period, but the average brick size of 15″×9″×2½″ indicates that it might pre-date the Chalukyan period. But further evidence is necessary to take it to this earlier date.

This earth-work is still in use and hence it gives an excellent idea about the use of the earth-works, that were thrown across streams and built water reservoirs. Such a system was widely prevalent in Gujarat at least from 1st millennium B. C. and continued for a very long time. At present also this system seems to be under effective operation in certain parts of the country.

Notes

[1] R. N. Mehta, 'Sudarsana Lake', *Journal of the Oriental Institute*, **XVIII**. Nos. 1 & 2, 21 ff.

[2] R. N. Mehta & Priyabala Shah, 'Saurastra Na Ketalak Praeina Sthavs' (Guj.) *Vak*, 1. 56.

[3] R. N. , Mehta, 'Ancient Bunds in Sabarkantha District,' *Journal of the Oriental Institute*, **XII**, No. 4, 352 ff.

[4] R. N. Mehta, *op. cit.*

[5] R. N. Mehta & Priyabala Shah *op. cit.*

[6] Kaneval at Godhra.

[7] Vadatalav and Sukra talav at Champaner.

[8] Aparajitaprechi, 74, 34.

Early Historic Fortifications in the Ganga valley

by MADHUKAR SHRIPAD MATE

Like so much else in the life of ancient India, the art of fortification was nurtured in its infancy by the Ganga valley. This remark necessarily excludes the achievements of the Harappans in this direction. The chronological and cultural void is great and if the various peoples and cultures that succeeded the Harappans knew or remembered anything of the massive ramparts and walls of such cities as Harappa or Mohenjodaro or Kalibangan, they did not leave behind them any material evidence of such knowledge. It would, therefore, be quite justifiable to describe the activity in this field during the latter three-quarters of the first millennium B. C. in the Ganga valley as a rebirth of military architecture on the continent. It is intended here to reexamine the remains of some nine sites in the Ganga valley and its periphery (Fig. 1) with a view to understand the growth and evolution of the art of fortification in ancient India.

Such an investigation shows that fortifications as a device of military utility came into being in this region not earlier than the fifth century B. C. It further shows that scholars have somehow shunned from the idea of making a distinction between an embankment and a rampart, thereby confusing the history of military architecture. The only noteworthy exception is that of Rajghat. The excavators of this site have after detailed investigations arrived at the conclusion that the mud-ramparts they had found and had once considered to be defensive works were in fact embankments meant to resist floods. And they have clearly said so. It would be practically impossible for anybody to escape the similarity in the materials and methods used at Rajghat on the one hand and those of Kausambi and Ujjain on the other. It seems fairly clear that Kausambi and Ujjain had embankments to begin with and only at a later date they were turned to military purposes with necessary modifications.

These conclusions are based mainly on three factors that have not received their due attention in earlier discussions. First and foremost is topography, the ups and downs and the folds of the land where the site existed. Next comes a comparison of various aspects present at the particular site and various features that should be or should not be there if it were to be a fortification. In other words, considerations from the military angle have to be taken into account. Thirdly, sculptural and pictorial representations and descriptions from technical or semi-technical treatises can hardly be ignored. These have to be compared with each other and then with the ruins at these various places.

The study begins with detailed descriptions of the ramparts or fortifications as reported by the explorers and excavators. The sites examined are : Ujjain, Kausambi, Rajghat, Rajgir, Pataliputra, Ahichchhatra, Sravasti, New Rajgir and Vaisali in that order.

Ujjain (Madhya Pradesh) is situated on the eastern bank of the river Sipra[1]. A mud rampart erected here in Period I (c. 700 B.

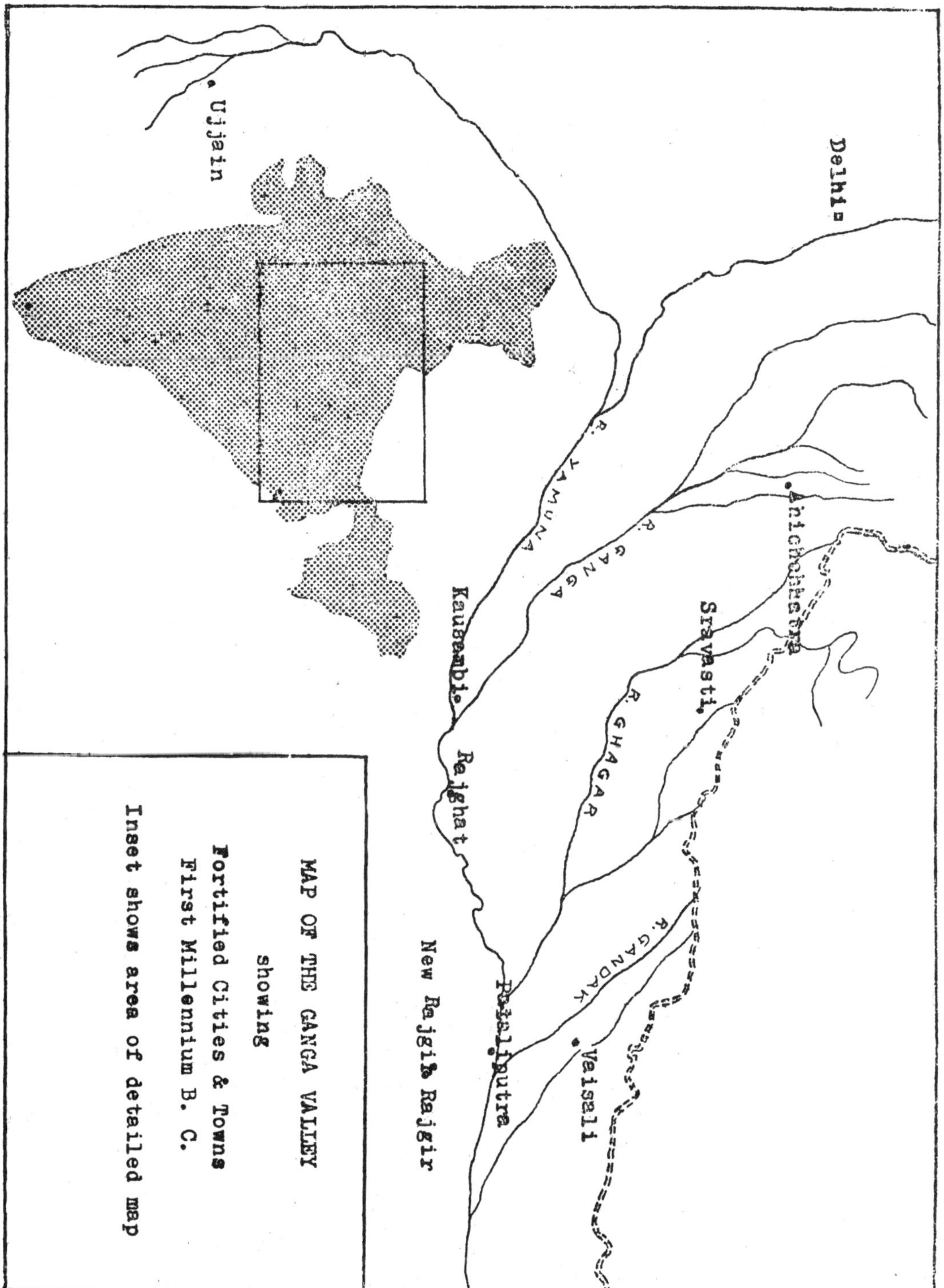

Figure 1 Map of the Ganga Valley.

C. to 500 B. C.) enclosed a polygonal area (Fig. 2). It was built by dumping the dug up yellow and black clays (from the moat) to form a thick wall with a gentle slope on the inner side and a less pronounced one on the other. This rampart had a basal width of bet-

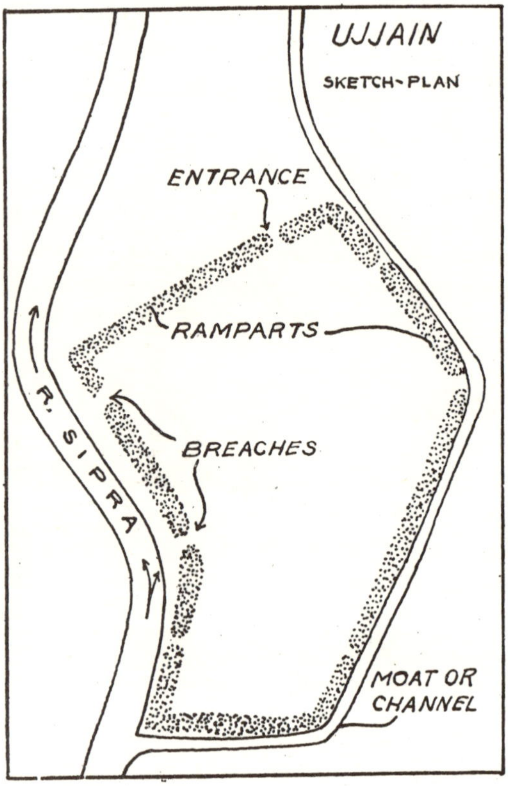

Figure 2 Ujjain : plan of ramparts.

ween 60 m. to 75 m. and its extant height is about 12 m. Immediately outside it and covering its southern and eastern sides was a moat between 23. 70 m. and 45 m. broad with a minimum depth of 6.50 m. To repair the damages to the rampart caused by the river floods, earthen fillings were given and then rivetted with burnt brick. The ramparts were also advanced riverwards and in so doing care was taken to reinforce them with stout timber logs.

This measure was visible for a length of 114 m. corresponding to the inward bend of the river. In this area the basal width of the rampart is as much as 105 m. In this same area the moat was lined by a brick wall to a depth of 8.10 m. The lining was on the side immediate to the mound. According to the excavator, during the succeeding three hundred years (c. 200 B. C. to 100 A. D.) the rampart continued to guard the city but fell in disuse after that. The major entrance to the city was through the north-western wall, the road was made of clay and pebbles and had to be resurfaced often.

Kausambi (District Allahabad) has been under excavation for over a decade now[2]. Information published on the remains at this site is available in plenty. However, it is piecemeal and no cogent picture emerges from it. This is mainly due to the failure on the part of the excavator to publish a comprehensive plan of the site indicating the mud-walls and ramparts, as has been most advisedly done in the case of Ujjain. Even the definitive report suffers from this lack. To a certain extent, Cunningham's sketch map[3] as well as the Survey of India sheets of the relevant area do step in to fill up this lacuna. (Fig. 3). The picture that can be made out of the mass of published details would be somewhat as follows.

Traces of the ancient habitation cover an area about eight square miles, a part of which was defended by a complex system of fortification. The mounds of the ancient rampart with the surrounding moat, form a semi-circle with the Yamuna as its base. The circuit of the ramparts is approximately six and a half km. The average height of the ramparts is 10.50 m. to 12.20 m. but nowhere is mention

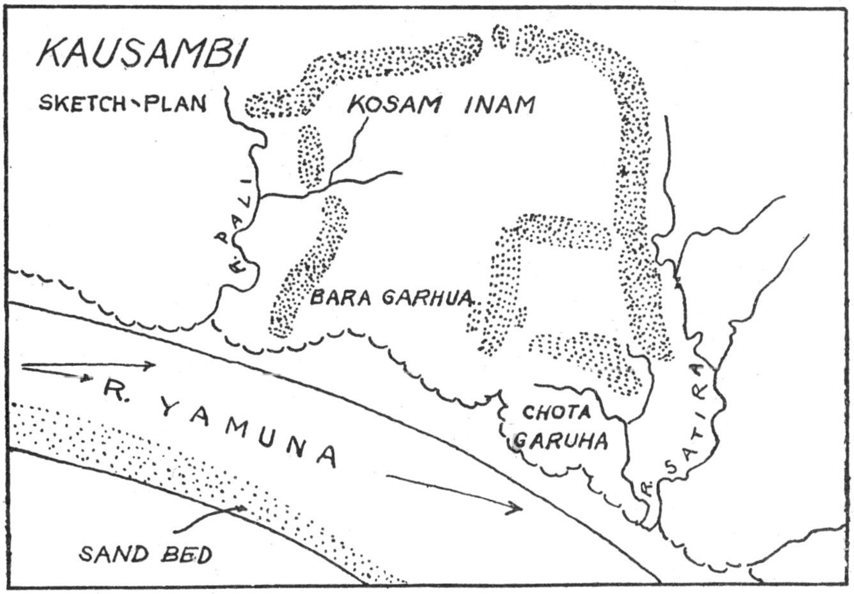

Figure 3 Kausambi : plan of the site and ramparts.

made of its basal width. Cunningham[4] also has expressed his inability to do it. Free standing towers measure from 21 m. to 22.70 m. in height. There are eleven gateways, five of which were principal ones, two in the east, two in the north and one in the west[5]. The moat surrounding the walls is supposed to be a later addition and has a width of from 120 m. to 300 m. at places. Except the construction of the towers, all the digging and building activity is assigned to Period I-originally dated 1,100 B.C., since revised to c. 8th-7th centuries B.C. The most striking feature, a brick revetment of 140 courses with a batter of 15 and 40 degrees given to the rampart is also ascribed to the same period.

In the subsequent periods subsidiary ramparts with basal widths of 9 m. to 5.20 m. were constructed. Their height was around 4.50 m. Brick towers were also erected over the earthen ones during this period. One such tower measured 11.40 m. x 5.20 m. and had projecting platforms on either sides with guard-rooms on the remaining two sides. A circular or curved brick wall and a corbelled drain have also been placed in this phase and although it has been hinted that they were in some way connected with the defences, no evidence to that effect has been offered. Excavations during 1962 are reported to have revealed a rather interesting feature : "The rampart on the southern side was found to have been made of mud. This wall evidently served a dual purpose viz. to defend the city in case of attack and save it from the floods of the Yamuna. The period of its construction and its subsequent history could not, however, be determined"[6]. Unless the factors that led to such a conclusion are revealed, justice cannot be done to the entire Kausambi data, for it speaks in two voices.

The remains of Rajghat (Dist. Varanasi) are spread over a triangular area between the rivers Ganga and Varuna (Fig, 4). The rampart was presumably built on natural soil and the extant height is 10 m. Remains of a platform in the form of stout timber logs and beams have been found near the toe of the rampart to a length of 34 m. Several deposits of sand and silt have been uncovered during the excavations. Here also no general plan has been published, nor details of the

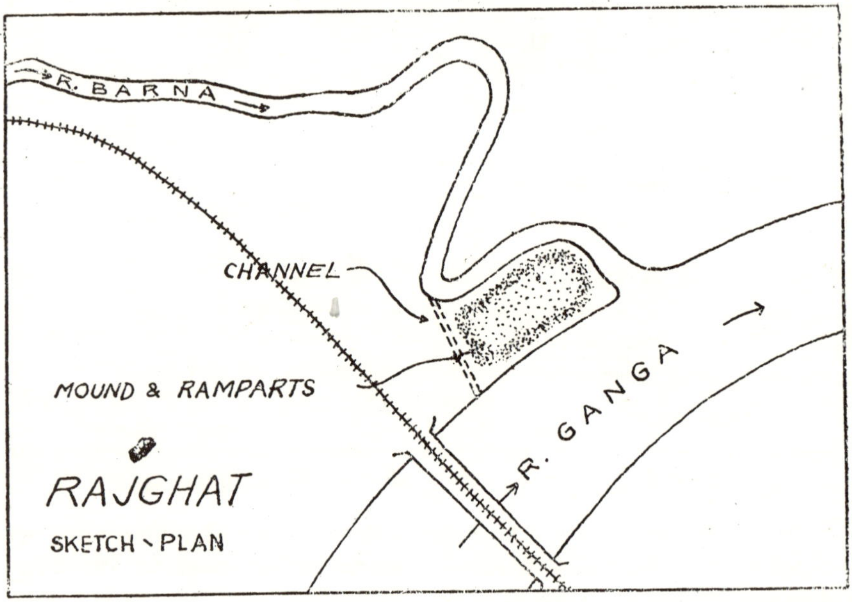

Figure 4 Rajghat : the site.

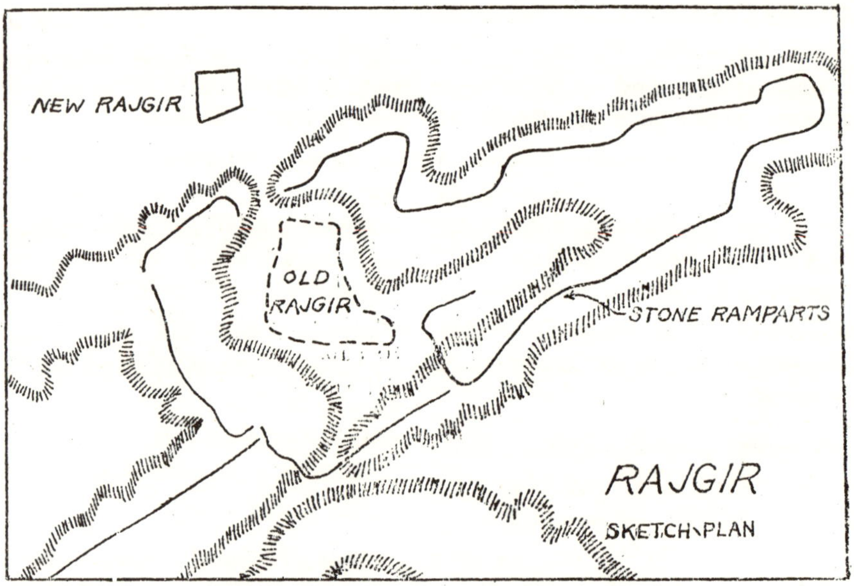

Figure 5 Rajgir and New Rajgir : plan.

basal width of the mud-rampart given. However, as stated earlier, the excavators have clarified the situation as under, "It was at this stage that a massive clay embankment was built as a defensive measure against the regular floods of the Ganga. Being merely a defensive measure against floods, it was not planned to be a regular fortification or rampart, a fact which is corroborated by three more cuttings laid in the same alignment"[7].

Rajgir (Dist. Patna, Bihar) was the capital of ancient Magadha or southern Bihar and is situated on the northern fringes of the Barbara hill ranges. The town itself is situated in a valley surrounded on all sides by hills. These hills provide an excellent natural fortification and shield it off from the plains of the north (Fig. 5)[8]. At a very early date in the life of the city the natural defences were substantially reinforced by a fortification consisting of a high rubble wall, generally 4 m. in thickness. It runs at the top of all the hills and has a circuit of about 40 km. The natural gaps between the hills were used as gates in the fortification. Inside this valley were other defensive walls built in different periods, the chief of which was the inner defensive wall, generally built of heaped up earth with pebble core and enclosing a pentagonal area with a perimeter of 8 km.

Pataliputra, modern Patna, the capital of Bihar, is situated on the confluence of the Son and the Ganga. It occupied a roughly triangular area of very narrow width (length 15 km. and breadth 2.5 km). The present city is located practically on the debris of the ancient settlement and large-scale excavations have not been possible. At a number of places structural remains have, however, been uncovered. "At Bulandibagh again, below some brick buildings of Gupta date, was found a unique wooden construction consisting of a series of 4.20 m. long wooden planks at the bottom, flanked by 4.50 m. high wooden uprights which were spanned on the top by tennoned planks, the entire arrangement making a hollow passage. This structure was uncovered to a length of 75 m. without reaching its end. It was identified as the wooden palisade mentioned by Megasthenes"[9]. A similar wooden structure, without, however, the bottom planks also came to light accidentally at Gosain-Khanda about three quarters of a kilometre from Bulandibagh. Megasthenes, the ambassador of Seleukos Nikator to the court of Chandragupta Maurya has left the following account. "It is in the shape of a parallelogram and is girdled with a wooden wall, pierced with loop-holes for the discharge of arrows. It has a ditch in front for defence for receiving the sewage of the city .... The ditch was 181 m. in breadth and 20 m. in depth... The wall had 570 towers and had sixty-four gates" [10]. How the timber structures found in the excavations and the descriptions of Megasthenes fit in with each other is to be seen slightly later on.

Ahichchhatra (Dist. Bareilly, U. P.) is presently enclosed by a fort wall with circular bastions 34 in number. This wall and the bastions are not more than three hundred years old, being built by Mughal officers of the region [11]. The circuit of these walls is 4.800 km. The shape of the area is roughly triangular (western side 915 m. northern 1.3 km. south-eastern 1.600 km). The place is situated between the rivers Ramaganga and Gangham which make access extremely difficult. On the eastern side is the Piriya Nala or Pairiya

River, also having steep banks and numerous deep pools of water. The remains of the ancient town are below this late medieval fortification and are described as under.

The town had a mud-rampart around it built in the Kushana period. In the second phase, it was considerably damaged and was therefore reinforced at the vertex by the construction of a brick-wall 4.98 m. broad and 2.59 m. high running throughout its length. (Earlier students had perceived two earlier ramparts in mud, over which, by the first century B. C., a brick wall was erected. But these observations now stand corrected as above.) "To economise the use of brick, rectangular gaps measuring 2.13 x 1.32 m. were left in the brick wall at regular intervals, and the openings filled with rubble and clay."[12] In the third phase the brick wall was given the protection of a mud cover as its first line of defence. It was buttressed in the fourth phase by another mud-packing. A partition wall has also been referred to in

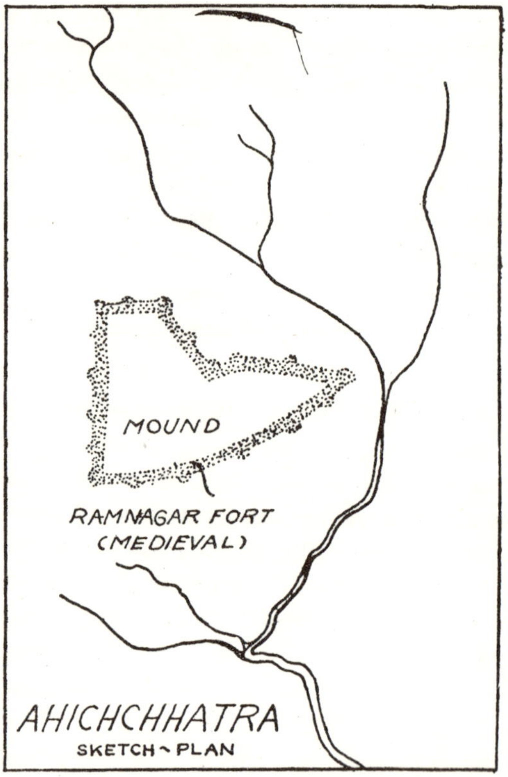

Figure 7 Ahichchhatra : general plan of the site.

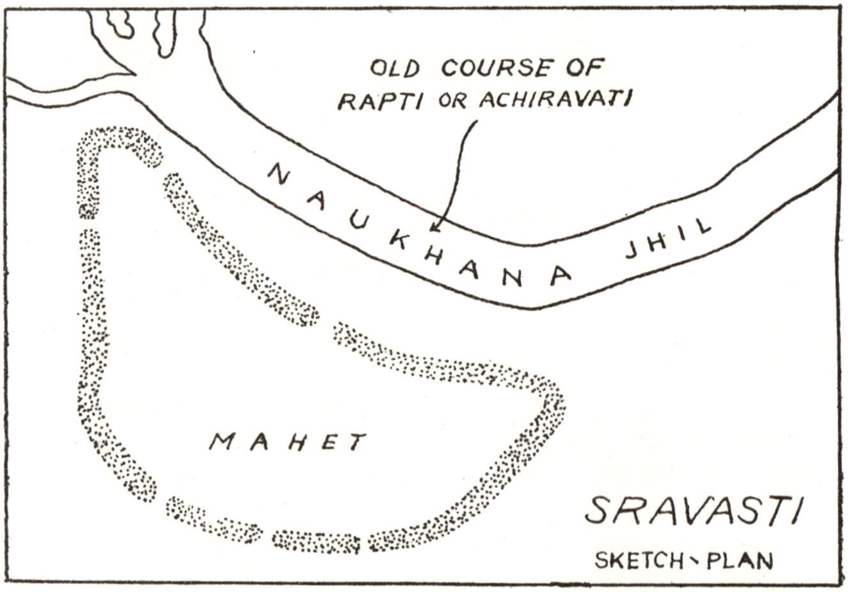

Figure 6 Sravasti : plan of the ramparts.

this connection, and it has been suggested that it divided the fortified area in two and the less secure portion was deserted (Fig. 6).

Sravasti (Dist. Bahraich, U. P.) is today represented by Mahet in the Baharaich and the Gonda districts of the U. P. [13]. It is on the southern bank of a sheet of water known as Naukhan Jhil which is a crescent-shaped inland lake. Cunningham, however, states specifically that it is the old course of the river Rapti, also known as Achiravati, which today flows about 2 km. north of the mound of Mahet[14]. The habitation at this place extended from the eighth cent. B. C. to fifty B. C. The area was girdled with a mud-wall about five km. in circuit by about 250 B. C. Its basal width is 29 m. and the extant height is 3.50 m. On its top, a brick structure 'serving probably as a parapet over the rampart' was erected. A mud filling was soon put over this and again a brick structure erected. All this activity is assigned to the period of 250 B. C. to 50 B. C. i.e. the Sunga and Kushana times (Fig. 7).

New Rajgir (Dist. Patna, Bihar) is a small fortified area outside the valley of Rajgir. The defence wall was hitherto believed to have been built of rubble. The excavations revealed a mud-rampart with a basal width of 40.33 m. except on the north where it is less by three metres, built over the remains of an N. B. P. habitation presumably destroyed by fire. Its extant height is 7.31 m. and on the southern side there was a brick-built retaining wall 2.13 m. in height, 1.21 m. wide at the top and with a batter. Outside it was a moat, the exact dimensions of which could be not ascertained. All this belonged to Period II A. A brick wall was added on the top (width of this wall is not mentioned)[15]. Over the collapsed debris of this wall a 2.13 m. thick deposit of earth and ash was laid in Period III A. Above this layer a wall of brick-bats was erected during Period III B. Its width was 3.35. m. Although the excavators do not offer precise dates, they suggest the sixth-fifth centuries B. C. as approximate dates for Period II, i. e. the beginning of the rampart. As to the rubble rampart suspected by previous investigators, it could not be traced in the area excavated.

Vaisali is today represented by Basarh in the Muzaffarpur district of Bihar (Fig. 8). The site was excavated several times. The work done during 1958-59 has revealed information highly valuable to the study of fortifications[16]. During Period I (Sunga, early second century B. C.) a wall of burnt bricks, perhaps 6 m. in thickness, was erected. In Period II i. e. the late second century B. C. a massive earthen rampart was superimposed on it. This had a basal width of 21 m. the extant top width was 6.30 m. and the extant height was 3.80 m. The digging of earth for this rampart naturally left around it a moat. During the late Kushana or early Gupta period (Period III) a burnt brick wall 2.70 m. in width was built on top of this earthen rampart.

Topography of each of these sites may now be examined in some detail. Ujjain is on the eastern bank of the Sipra river. The river has a typical 'S' shaped bend here and flowing south to north as it does; if in spate it would burst right in the heart of the city. Especially the banks opposite the point where the course turns northwest at a sharp angle would be vulnerable to the pressure of mounting waters. Just before the S bend begins, a moat has been dug towards the east. Running about 700 m. due east it turns towards the

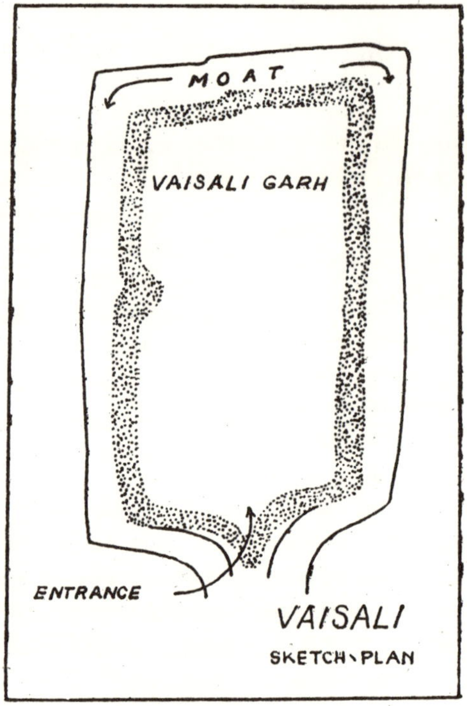

FIG. 8

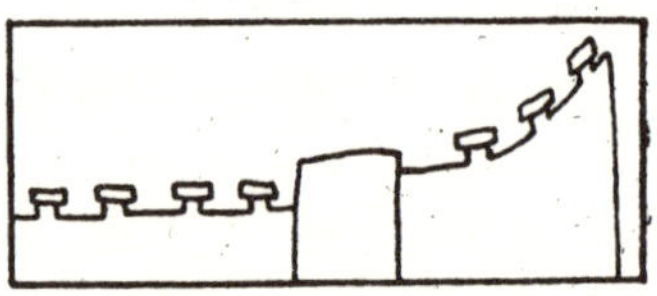

SANCHI: RAMPARTS

AMRAVATI: GATEWAY

SANCHI : GATEWAY

BODHGAYA: PARAPETS

FIG. 9

Figure 8. Vaisali : plan of Vaisali Garh. Figure 9. Sanchi : ramparts. Sanchi : gateway. Bodh Gaya : parapets. Amravati : gateway.
All these are line drawings and sketches made from plans and photographs published in works cited in the references. They do not have any scale.

north-east. After going in that direction for a distance of 900 m. it changes direction again to flow north-westwards and then eventually meets the river. The width and depth of the moat leave little doubt that it was intended as a diversion channel to carry off excess water during floods thus considerably reducing the force of the main stream of the Sipra before it reached Ujjain. That it did often enter the city is shown by the wide breaches seen in the western side of the rampart. It was at these various points and the south-western tip that brick revetments and timber reinforcements were found. Many of the breaches as well as the moat were filled up (in antiquity) by erosional deposits. The location of the gate provides, if additional proof were required, a certain indication. It is located in the northern wall in the north-eastern corner. It opens on a patch of ground which is comparatively away from the river and her floods.

Next to be reviewed is the position of Kausambi. It has been identified with the area presently embracing Kosam Inam, Garhua-Barha and Garhua Chota. On the western side of this area the river Pali and its tributary streamlets form deep channels. On the eastern side the river Satira and its tributary streams form equally deep channels. Towards the north no such natural gulley entirely covering this piece of land is visible, but the tributaries of Pali and Satira close in on each other and leave only a small belt free of water. The Yamuna here flows in a south-easterly direction. The southern bank is gradually sloping and huge sand-beds lie immediately close to it. Water could spread over here effortlessly. The northern bank is steep and takes the full force of the onrushing waters. The numerous gullies seen on this side are beds of streams running towards the the river under normal conditions. However, during conditions of heavy flooding, water of the river enters them to flood the whole area turning the Pali and the Satira into dangerous neighbours. The thick burnt-brick revetment, the constant advancement of the ramparts in this area and mud-rampart on the southern side of the town would indicate this to be the case.

At Rajghat the excavators have clearly stated that the mud ramparts discoverd at that place were embankment to resist the encroachment of flood waters. For a place like Rajghat that would be subject to flooding from two directions, the north and the south, a massive embankment along with moats and diversion channels was the only protection. Although the northern portion of this site has not been subjected to thorough excavations, a moat has been traced.

Pataliputra did not possibly fair as well as the three sites mentioned above. Its position is definitely precarious. Floods must have been a constant source of danger. The excavated ruins in the form of timber verticals and beams across them were most probably the inner core of a huge earthen rampart. They might have or might not have formed an enclosed passage within the rampart but they certainly served as reinforcements. It is most likely that on top of this earthen rampart timber parapets and wall of which Megasthenes speaks were erected. These parapets would shield the archers posted to defend the city. This is the only explanation that would account for all the known facts of topography, of archaeology and of history. Pataliputra could thus very well be treated as the first (known) step towards the transformation of flood embankments into military structures.

Sravasti might represent a similar phenomenon. Its proximity to the river Rapti and the curved course of that river would have exposed the town to periodic floods. And hence the first wall might have become necessary. The basal width of 29 m. makes it appear as if it was intended to avert floods; human beings could be and were excluded with much thinner walls. The brick parapet wall above this embankment might be a later addition or if the two were contemporary, Sravasti walls should be treated as double purpose walls. If, however, the Rapti had already started changing its course by the time Sravasti started flourishing such an embankment would be unnecessary.

Ahichchhatra, New Rajgir and Vaisali do not face this problem. The rivers flowing past them are at a very safe distance and even in spates would not encroach upon any of these sites. There is no need in their case of any flood protection measures.

It has been shown above that the massive mudwalls reinforced by timber and externally revetted with burnt brick could be interpreted as embankments meant to resist floods at least in the case of half the number of sites considered. Their substantial sizes involve tremendous labour and utilization of men and material on a truely vast scale. Such an effort would be undertaken by any society only if it is faced with a problem of such immense magnitude. An invading army need not have a rampart of 75 m. basal width or a succession of subsidiary ramparts as wide when put together. The same is true of the so-called moats with widths of 30 m. and above and reaching to 300 m. in the case of Kausambi at one place. These would be more appropriately called diversion channels. The brick-revetments with the particular angle of batter as at Kausambi would be an invitation to an invading army, they could be easily scaled in a mass sortie. But floods would be prevented from eroding the embankment by these revetments. Again, Ujjain, Kausambi or Rajghat have no traces of any parapets above the ramparts. They are a cardinal military requirement, in their absence, it would be merely shifting the battle-ground from a plain to a mound. That element provided by the mason which stands between the assualt party and the defenders, which shields the latter while enabling them to throw missiles on the former, viz. the parapets, is totally absent in all these three sites. Militarily they are next to useless.

In contrast, the later towns have mud-walls of much smaller dimensions and have, as a rule, brick or timber as at Pataliputra parapets over them. By the third century B. C. it had become axomatic that there must be such a parapet. The *Arthaśāstra*[17] most faithfully records this practice when it says :

"At a distance of four *daṇḍas* from the moat, he should cause a rampart to be made out of the earth dug out, six *daṇḍas* high, made compact..."and" on top of the rampart he should cause a parapet to be built, double the breadth in height, built of bricks... with the top decked with drums or monkey heads"

It would become clear that the brick wall on top of the Ahichchhatra rampart is not, as the excavators have made out, a later addition, but is a part and parcel of the earliest fortification. It runs all along the rampart and if it could have been found intact, there is little doubt it would have shown the monkey-heads or *kapi-śirṣas* of the parapets. From available archaeological data it would appear that ruins from Ahichchhatra could be treated as the earliest remains of a military fortification from the Ganga valley and that it was followed close on its heels by New Rajgir and Vaisali. Pataliputra and Rajgir might be contemporaries. As to the general aspect of these ancient fortifications representations on the sculptures at Bodhgaya, Sanchi and Amaravati[18], though slightly later in date, would be most illustrative. All of them (Fig. 9) show brick walls with parapets or *kapi-śirṣas* of various designs. And although nothing regarding the maots or the mud-ramparts could be deduced from them, they are of great value in another direction. None of the above excavations, tell anything about the gateways or entrance structures. These sculptures could step in and impart a good idea of the nature and appearance of gateways etc.

To sum up, from the examination of the excavated remains of nine of the most well-known sites of the Ganga valley, it seems that the earlier ones have embankments and diversion channels meant as flood protection devices whereas the ones that came into prominence during the fifth century B. C. and onwards had formidable fortification around them. And this conclusion has to be stated inspite of all literary evidence cited on this subject so far[19].

Notes

[1] *Indian Archaeology-A Review, (IAR)*, 1955 to 58.

[2] G. R. Sharma, *The Excavation at Kausambi, 1957-59*; (Allahabad), 1960. 27-40. and *I A R*, 1960-61 to 64-65.

[3] A. Cunningham, *Archaeological Survey of India Reports*, Vol. 1. Pl. XLVIII.

[4] *Ibid.*

[5] Sharma, *op. cit.* [2].

[6] *I A R*—1962-63, 33.

[7] *I A R*—1957-58 and 1960-61 to 64-65; 1964-65, I-81.

[8] A. Ghosh, "Rajgir : 1950", *Ancient India*, No. 7, 66-78. and *I A R*—1956-57, 1958-59.

[9] Y. D. Sharma, "Exploration of Early Historical Sites", *Ancient India*, No. 9, 147.

[10] J. W. McCrindle, *"Ancient India as described by Megasthenes and Arrian*, (Calcutta), 1926, 65.

[11] Cunningham, *op. cit.*, 255-265. ; I A R—1963-64, 44.

[12] *I A R*—1963-64, 44.

[13] *I A R*—1957-58, 47-50.

[14] Cunningham, op. cit., 331.

[15] *I A R*—1961-62, 7-8.

[16] *I A R*-1957-58 to 61-62; 1958-59, 12 and K. Deva and V. Misra, *Vaisali Excavations, 1960.*

[17] R. P. Kangle, *Kautiliya Arthashastra*, Vol II, 71-72. (Bombay), 1963.

[18] Bodhgaya : L. Bachhofer, *Early Indian Sculpture*, 42.

Amaravati : *Ibid*, 123.

Sanchi : H. Zimmer, *Art of Indian Asia*, 2, Pls 9 & 18.

[19] S. D. Singh, *Ancient Indian Warfare with special reference to the Vedic Period*; (Leiden), 1965, 119-134.

A Middle Stone Age Site on River Durgawati in District Shahabad, Bihar

by BHUPENDRA PAL SINGH

In the last few years after independence archaeological activities in Bihar attracted a lot of attention of the scholarly world with the discovery of Stone Age tools and Historical material [1]. Ironically enough, these activities are confined mostly in the north-eastern and south-eastern parts of the province, leaving Shahabad district a *terra incognita*. Very little we know about the prehistory of the district, which incidently lies on the borders of one of the prehistorically richest regions of India i. e., Mirzapur. The Kaimur running through district Mirzapur extends eastward to the district Shahabad of Bihar, thus forming a physiographically distinct region in an identical geological frame work. Mirzapur had yielded rich evidence of more than one prehistoric cultures. Shahabad too, if explored exhuastively, is bound to provide the glimpses of the cultural milieu of Stone Age societies and also the extent of their nomadic wanderings in the eastern Kaimurs.

The present note records the first discovery of a few Middle Stone Age tools in the district, which were collected by the author near Malhipur in Sasaram sub-division along the left bank of river Durgawati. Besides, a rich Late Stone Age [2] industry near Gupteshwar and several Black-and-red and N. B. P. yielding sites on both the sides of the river were also found [3].

The river Durgawati rises at Bhakma on the southern ridge of the plateau. After passing through the vicinity of the Stalactite caves of the Gupteshwar and hill fortress of Shergarh, it enters the plains at Karamchat and flows towards Jahanabad and ultimately falls into the Karamnasa in the north-east after recieving the Kudra in the east. Malhipur is situated in the middle reaches. Here the river has been narrowed by the continuous deposit of sand, occasionally covered with gravels. The tools under study are found in these gravels.

Of the numerous stratigraphical sub-divisions constituting the Vindhyan System only three are conspicuous by their presence in the area, viz. Kaimur Sandstone, the Bijaigarh Shales and the Rohtas Limestone. Rohtas Limestone, which is exposed here, has a aggregate thickness of five feet, and supplies the silicious material [4]. It is these nodules which are picked up from the river bed and utilized in the fabrication of Middle and Late Stone Age tools in the valley. The famous stalactite caves of Gupteshwar are situated in this limestone belt.

As regards the stratigraphy, no section of definite antiquity is found exposed on the river banks. At places, a layer of gravel of varying thickness is seen embedded in the cliff. The probable sequence of deposit from top to bottom in the Durgawati, made out after much searching, seems to be as follows:

(1) Brownish red clay

(2) Gravel

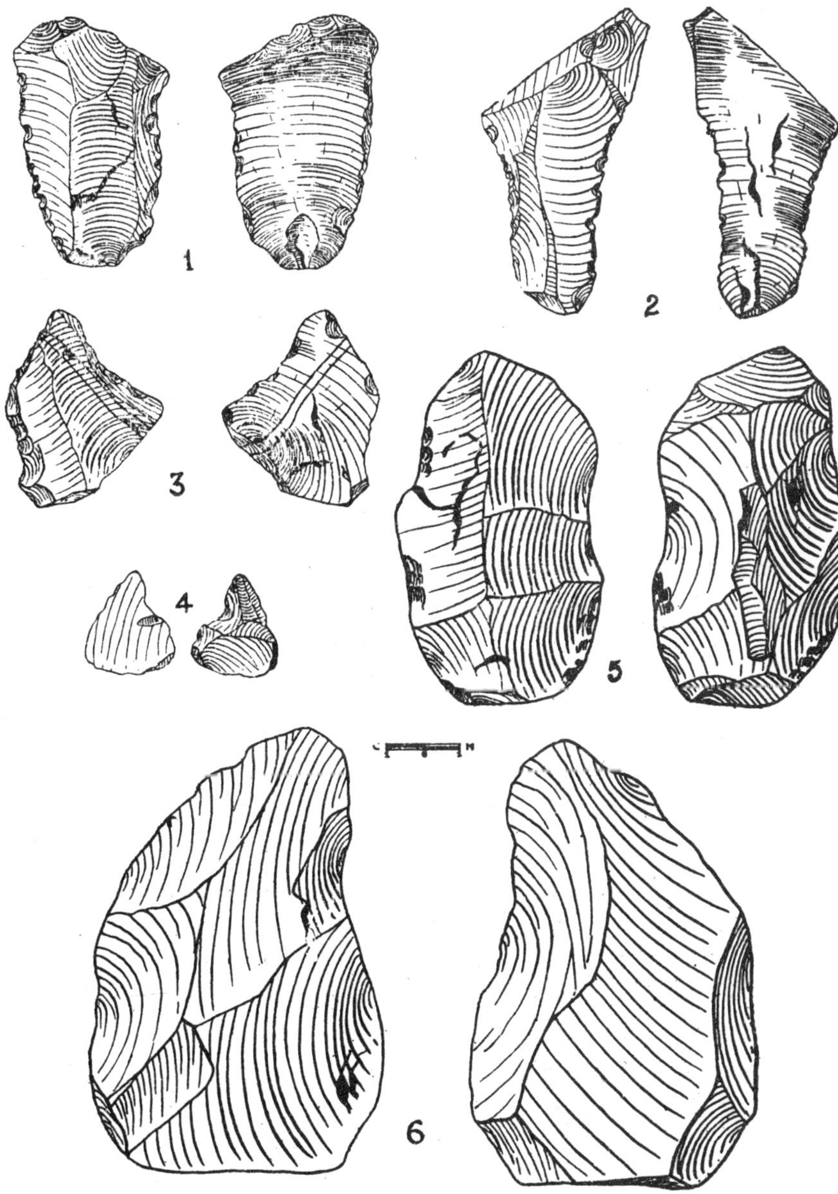

(Fig 1) Middle Stone Age Tools from Shahabad.

(3) Silt

(4) Kankar.

All the tools are picked up from the gravel of the river bed and have not lost their original lustre and freshness, except two specimens in which some rolling is evident. The absence of definite stratigraphic sequence, so also the small number of the tools in the loose gravel support the chance of their transportation from some full fledged site which perhaps lies in the nearby hills. The raw material used for the tools is invariably silicious and mostly flint.

All the implements but one have been made on flakes and having a faceted platform. They have a soft diffused bulb of percussion, sometimes with a tiny flat bulbar scar, which attest the use of soft stone hammer. Mostly flakes of the collection exhibit Levallois tendency. One flake of the collection (Fig. 1) shows careful preparation of core before being detached It is a typical Levallois flake. One single specimen of thick quartzite flake was also found If the size and crudeness of technique are any criteria, the specimen should be assigned to the Early Stone Age. Typo-technologically, these tools appear to be in full agreement with the Middle Stone Age tools of Mirzapur [5]. The length of artifacts varies from 2.6. cms. to 8.2 cms.

The typo-technological description of the tools is as follows :

1. (Fig. 1,1) A side scraper on roughly subtriangular flake of Levallois type, which has been flaked from its underside, and on the shorter end. The marks of the preparation of the core are present on both the ends. Both the lateral margins are partially retouched from the vertical surface. The retouch is short, although not very regular. Under surface is plain with a weak bulbar-scar. State of preservation is fresh. Dark flint.

2. Fig. 1,2 A thick blade with a narrow base and a broken soft bulb and broad head. It is interesting to note that the specimen contains striking platforms on both the ends–the upper one is plain but unprepared and the lower one is faceted. Marks of use are visible on both the edges. The cross-section is triangular. State of preservation-fresh. Brownish flint.

3. (Fig. 1,3) A rolled triangular flake, which, on the basis of the shape and preparation of striking platform may be compared with so-called pseudo-Levallois point. The edges show some dull and faint retouch marks at high angle. Dark grey flint.

4. (Fig. 1,4) A piece of a broken flake, with a notch formed as a result of fine retouch at a high angle. State of preservation-fresh. Dark black flint.

5. (Fig. 1,5) An elongated and rectangular core from which some large flakes have been removed haphazardly. State of preservation—rolled. Brownish-yellow opal.

6. (Fig. 1,6) Irregular flake of fine grained quartzite. Four big flakes have been removed from the upper surface, while three from the under surface. Slightly rolled. Typologically belongs to the Early Stone Age.

Notes

[1] B. P. Sinha, Presidential address in the Seminar on Pottery at Patna, 1968.

[2] B. P. Singh, "A microlithic site from Shahabad (Bihar), *Purātattva*, Vol. I, 100-103, Pl. XII, 1967-68.

[3] B. P Singh, "Exploration in Shahabad (Bihar)", 14-50, 1968, unpublished Report—Copy in the Department of A. I. H. C. and Archaeology, B. H. U.

[4] E. Vredenberg, "Suggestion for the classification of the Vindhyan System" *Rec. Geol. Surv. Ind.*, Vol. 38, 255-60, 1906.

[5] B. P. Singh, "Stone Age Industries on Balia Nadi, Mirzapur". 80-84, 1962, unpublished M. A. thesis, copy in the Department of Anthropology, Lucknow University, Lucknow.

A Sealing from Sunet and Saiva Vaishnava Syncretism

by KIRAN KUMAR THAPLYAL

Sectarian jealousies and rivalries often prompted the followers of various sects to create pieces of visual arts to glorify their own deities and show their superiority over those of the others. Such tendencies were more prominent amongst the followers of Śaivism and Vaishṇavism within the Hindu fold, as demonstrated by such icon-types as Nṛi-siṁha and Śarabha [1]. Yet certain icon-types like Hari-Hara and Trimūrti clearly show that attempts were also made at rapprochement between the two. The present unpublished sealing from Sunet (District Ludhiana), now in the Indian Museum, Calcutta [2], belongs to the latter type (Pl.IV B).

The clay sealing is circular in shape and bears in the upper field a *triśūla* and a conventionalized *chakra* and, in the lower, a neatly executed legend *Śri-Dvipārshadasya* in Gupta characters.

The word *pārshada'* means an associate, companion or attendant especially of some god [3]. The legend *Dvipārshadasya* means '(seal) of one who has two *pārshadas*'. The two *pārshadas* in the present context undoubtedly refer to the *Triśūla* and *chakra*, the *āyudhas* of Śiva and Vishṇu respectively. It is only Hari-Hara–a form representing the ideal union of Vishṇu and Śiva that can claim to have the *Triśūla* and the *chakra* as *pārshadas*. The sealing, in all probability, belonged to some temple enshrining Hari-Hara type of cult icon in its *sanctum sanctorum.*

Sunet, so well known for Yaudheva coin-moulds, has yielded a large number of seals and sealings and other antiquities, some of them unmistakably religious in character. Some sealings from that site in the Indian Museum, Calcutta, bear distinct Śaiva devices. One [4] has the lone symbol of *triśūla*, another [5] a *triśūla* and *nandi* while yet another [6] a *triśūla* and the legend *Rudraśarma* on the obverse, the reverse bearing the same symbol with the legend *Jajjasya.* Still another [7] has a *triśūla-paraśu* and a vase.

We have also Vaishṇava sealings from this site. One in the Indian Museum, Calcutta [8] has a *śaṅkha* on pedestal and the legend *Śrīdevasya* in Gupta characters. Typically Vaishṇavite is the sealing from this site bearing the legend *Śri jitaṁ bhagavatā svāmi Nārāyaṇena* [9] (victory has been achieved by the Lord Nārāyaṇa) which compares favourably with such other Vaishṇava legends as *jitaṁ bhagavatā* [10], *jitaṁ bhagavatā Vāsudevena* [11] and *jitaṃ bhagavatā gataghana gaganābhena* [12] occuring on seals and in epigraphs. The evidence thus suggests the coexistence of Śaiva and Vaishṇava cults.

Our sealing is not the lone example testifying to the combined form of Vishṇu and Śiva (Hari-Hara). We may refer to a clay sealing from this very site and in the Indian Museum, Calcutta [13], bearing a *triśūla* and the legend *Mātriśarma* in Gupta characters on one side and the device of a *chakra* on the other. Still morespecific in this context are a good number of sealings hailing from this site and bearing the legend *Śaṅkara-Nārāyaṇābhyāṁ* '(Salutations to Śaṅkara and Nārāyaṇa) in Gupta characters. These [14] do not bear string-marks and instead contain either finger-impressions or the name of some individual (devotee) and were, therefore, votive-offerings to some shrine dedicated to Śaṁkara and Nārāyaṇa or tokens offered as *prasāda* by the priests of such a shrine. The above cited evidence clearly contradicts the assertion of J. Agrawal that Sunet had no devotional traditions [15].

The sealing under discussion probably also belonged to the same temple as those with the legend *Śaṅkara-Nārāyaṇābhyāṁ* and one bearing Śaiva and Vaishṇava devices on its two sides, referred to above. Syncretistic icons are met with from the Kushāṇa period onwards [16] and the religious catholicity of the Imperial Guptas, during whose rule the present sealing was manufactured, no doubt, added greater fillip to the creation of such images.

ACKNOWLEDGEMENT

The author is grateful to the authorities of the Indian Museum, Calcutta, for facilities of study and photograph of the seal.

Notes

[1] Vishṇu in the form of Nṛisiṁha killed Hiraṇyakaśipu, the devotee of Śiva (and thus protected his own devotee Prahlāda).

[ ] Indian Museum, No. 4624-A12823.

[3] See Monier Williams, *Sanskrit English Dictionery*, *S. V.*

[4] Indian Museum, No. 4692-A 12871.

[5] Indian Museum, No. 4699-12878.

[6] Indian Museum, No. 4680-12864.

[7] Indian Museum, No. 4695-A 12874.

[8] Indian Museum, No. 4677-12862.

[9] G. B. Sharma, 'Sealings from Sanghol and Sunet', *JNSI*, XXX, 220-22, at p. 222 and pl. XIII, 4.

[10] *Jitaṁ bhagavatā* occurs on an agate seal-stamp found on a hill close to Parsenoi near Nagpur (*JNSI*, III, 100); on Nos. 33, 34, 35 and 36 of Bloch's list of Basarh seals (*ASIAR*, 1903-04, 111) and on certain seals found at Oceo (A. H. Dani, *Indian Palaeography*, 228). Cf. also Narasaropet Copper-plate Inscription of Siṁhavarman (D. C. Sircar, *Select Inscriptions*, 2nd ed., 469).

[11] This legend occurs on a clay seal in the collection of Shri R. C. Tandon, Allahabad. See *JNSI*, XXIX, 27.

[12] Penukonda Copper-plate Inscription of Madhava, *Select Inscriptions*, 2nd ed., 480.

[13] Indian Museum, No. 4624-A 2823.

[14] E. J. Rapson, 'Notes on Indian Coins and Seals, Part IV, Indian Seals and Clay Impressions', *JRAS*, 1901, 97-108, Nos. 1 and 2 and pl. facing p. 98, Nos. 1 and 2 J. Agrawal has published three sealings from this very site with this legend on one side and *Śrī Mātriśarmaṇaḥ* on the other, ('Some clay sealings from Sunet,' *JNSI*, XX, 66-68). We have noticed more than two dozen sealings bearing this

legend in the Indian Museum, Calcutta, of of which a few may be referred to here. No. 4651—A 12850 has the legend *Mātriś-arma* No. 4650-12849 *Śrī-Vishṇudāsasya*, Nos. 4640-12848 and 4652-12851 have *Mānyah*. The legend *Śāṅkara-Nārāyaṇābh-yāṁ* also occurs on certain sealings in the Allahabad Museum, e. g., Nos. 266, 271, 292 etc.

[15] J. Agrawal, 'An Interesting Clay Sealing from Sunet', *JNSI*, XIX, 71-72. It was because of this belief that Agrawal did not accept the suggestion of taking the legend *Dharma karavya* on some Sunet sealings to 'have a purely devotional significance' and instead suggested that the legend refers to the 'resolve of the Yaudheyas to continue their fight against the Kushāṇas till victory was achieved (see *ibid.*, p. 70, text and fn.).

[16] See J. N., Banerjea, *Development of Hindu Iconography* (2nd ed.). 121 ff.

Archaeological Explorations in Basti District (U.P.)

by S. K. BHATT

Basti, like many other districts of India, is an administrative headquarters created by the British. In eighteenth century A. D. its existence was simply as a village. As the name itself indicates, it was populated by a few families at first but afterwards, as it seems, it began to take a bigger and wider shape and in 1801 A. D. it was selected as a tahsil headquarters of Gorakhpur district [1]. Later on, in 1865, it was declared as a separate district, lying between 26° 25′ and 27° 30′ north latitude and 82° 13′ and 82° 10′ east longitude. It comprises a tract of irregular shape. The length from north to south varies between 52 to 68 miles and the breadth from east to west ranges from 28 to 52 miles. The total area is 2795.5 sq. miles [2].

The boundaries of Basti district are formed by an international agreement on the north and a natural demarcation formed by river Ghaghara on the south. Its northern boundary is formed by a long tract of land, about 80 ft. in width, in the middle of which runs a series of brick-built columns. But its eastern and western boundaries are purely administrative ones. On the west lies the district Gonda and to the east is Gorakhpur district. On the south the river Ghaghara separates it from Fyzabad, while on the north the boundary touches with Nepal running at a distance of 20 or 30 miles from the outer range of the Himalayas.

So far as the archaeological explorations and excavations are concerned, unfortunately the district has been comparatively neglected. For the first time A. C. L. Carlleyle [3]explored a few sites of archaeological importance in 1874-75 and 1875-76, under the guidance of A. Cunningham. Subsequently in 1890 Fuhrer [4] explored a few more sites and published his list adding some more information. In February, 1897 V. A. Smith suspected Piparahava to be a stupa and told Mr. Peppe that relics would be found at about the ground level [5]. In the subsequent year Peppe excavated it and the famous Piparahava vase, containing Buddha's relics, beads, crystals, gold ornaments, cut-stars etc. was unearthed [6]. Later on, a few more exploration and excavations were undertaken by P. C. Mukherjee [7] in Nepal frontier in the year 1899. Then there is a big gap as no further interest was shown to conduct any exploration in the area.

No doubt, these archaeologists did much effort to find out and locate the sites but they were only partly successful in their efforts. The pottery evidence was totally neglected as it was not known to these archaeologists. So they fully depended upon literary evidences and stone objects, sculptures, inscriptions, and coins found from the mounds.

The information supplied by these archaeologists is also some times not correct. In this connection the statement of Carlleyle and Fuhrer regarding the location and identification of Hathikunda can be cited as one example [8]. The Nirvan Stupa of Konagamana as described by Fuhrer is another example of incorrect identification of an archaeological monument [9].

Many of the sites and the Stupas, which have been explored by Carlleyle and Fuhrer, are not tracable now because of heavy rain-fall in the region. Many sites are disturbed by the villagers for the cultivation and quarrying of bricks. The identification of many historical sites mentioned in the Buddhist texts by Carlleyle and Fuhrer have been contradicted now. For example Carlleyle located Kapilavastu at Bhuiladih [10] and Rummindei near Sheopur [11] or between Sheopur and Budhapar, both in the southern part of Basti District, but nowadays both are identified with Tilaurakot and Rummindei situated in Nepal border.

Again in 1962-63 a team of Banaras Hindu University explored parts of Basti District under the supervison of A. K. Narain assisted by P. C. Pant, and a few more new sites were brought to light [12].

After 1964 the author started a village to village survey of the district and adjoining area in connection with his doctoral thesis on 'The Archaeology of Basti District from Early Times to 1200 A. D.' As a result, altogether sixty-seven archaeological sites were discovered which yielded the characterstic ceramic industries of the early historic period besides coins and other small antiquities (See Table). The most important site amongst these is Gularihavāghāt (lat. 27° 47′ N. long. 82° 28′ E.) which was discovered in Harraiya Tahsīl on the left bank of the river Manorama in Dec. 1967. From the surface explorations the site yielded the following ceramic industries :—

1. Black-and-Red Ware : both plain and painted (white on black and black on red surface in the case of paintings)
2. Black Slipped Ware : plain and painted (white and black, in both pigments)
3. Grey Ware.
4. N. B. P. and associated red ware.
5. Red ware of varied fabric and type.

1. Black-and-Red Ware

The finding of Black-and-Red Ware at Gularihavāghāt adds a new name to the group of the sites yielding the said ware in the Gangetic plain. If the migratory pattern of Black-and-Red Ware suggested by D. P. Agrawal [13] is considered in the light of our evidence, it will not be improper if the arrow from Chirand going to Rajghat is turned via Gularihavāghāt in Basti.

Black-and-Red Ware of the site shows a poor texture of less lavigated clay which also contains husk, mica and sand. Pots are wheel-made.

A. Plain Black-and-Red Ware : the fabric of the plain Black-and-Red ware industry leads to categorize it as following :—

i. Coarse fabric : The clay of the sherds belonging to this category is very coarse and micaceous, the firing has resulted in two zones, black and red, in the core. The outer surface of almost all sherds is treated with red wash. There are a few sherds only to show the application of the red slip. The interior of the sherds has no surface treatment. A few sherds have mat impression over the outer surface.

ii. Medium fabric : Sherds in this group are treated with slip on both sides. Numerous small cavities in the core suggest its high porosity. The core is dominated by black zone due to the use of husk. In these specimens the potter has taken much care about the surface treatment.

iii. Fine fabric : Sherds of this group are not so fine as the south Indian Megalithic Black-and-Red Ware, but it is finer in Gularihavāghāt Black-and Red ware industry. Sherds are well fired with red slip applied on the outer surface. The fine fabric sherds give metallic ring. The clay is less porous and mica becomes rare. The core of the sherds is tough and hard with prominent red zone.

SHAPES

VASES : long, featureless and sometimes thickened rim, carination near the neck.

BOWLS : straight and convex sided.

DISH ON STAND : The stand is hollow and long with greyish core and red slip on outer surface. The inner portion and rim is black due to inverted firing. The dish is similar to shallow bowl, the inner portion and the rim portion is black and outer portion is red. Sometimes it is treated with red slip also.

B. Painted Black-and-Red ware : This group of potsherds is similar to the preceding group in its clay, surface treatment and the technique of firing but a few specimens of fine texture are also noticed. The pots are also wheel-made and they differ from the former group having vertical, horizontal, criss-cross and zig-zag paintings done with the help of the brush. The outer surface is treated with red slip and painted in black. Sometimes the black pigment is used in paintings in inner portion on black washed surface. Paintings show a common use of white pigment also. The vertical lines are drawn from top to bottom resulting in thinner ends.

2. Black Slipped Ware

The black slipped ware industry of the site is both plain and painted. The clay and its texture, lavigation and firing are the same as reported from other sites in the Gangetic plain. The sherds are treated with black slip on both the sides. In comparison to the N. B. P. ware, these are thicker, having a little coarser texture. The core is generally black and sometimes greyish black. Paintings done with the help of brush, are linear in black and white pigments. The paintings comprise vertical and horizontal lines, criss-cross, zig-zag, and goemetrical designs having a regularity in their placement [4].

3. N. B. P. and Grey ware

These industries are very common on the site as well as in the district. The clay, lavigation, texture and fabric is the same as reported from the other sites of the Gangetic plain.

SHAPES :

Grey Ware :

BOWLS : convex sided sharpened rim

ii. Rounded side with sharpened rim.

iii. Straight side and sharpened rim.

DISHES : Shallow and short sharpened rim

ii. Incurved side with straight sharpened rim.

iii. Inturned featureless rim.

VASES : i. with outcurved rim bevelled at the top and concave constricted neck.

BASINS : i. convex side with outcollared rim.

ii. rounded side with elliptical rim.

SHAPES IN N. B. P. WARE

BOWLS : i. flanged bowls with its variants.

ii. convex side with featureless and sharpened rim. flat base.

DISHES i. inturned featureless rim, convex side, sagger base.

ii. vertical, externally bevelled rim, slightly convex side.

4. RED WARE

This industry is reported from the site in its two stages :

(i) Pre- N. B P.

(ii) N. B. P. associate

Red ware of the pre-N. B. P. stage can be divided into three sub-groups on the basis of their surface treatment.

A. Slipped red ware : these are usually slipped on both the sides, but there are exceptions of only one side treatment also. The fabric is noticed both, medium and thick. There are stone particles and husk used as degrasent. Mica is prominently used. porosity in sherds is noticed by small cavities on the surface. Red zone is prominent in the core.

B. Washed red were : These are of medium fabric and well fired, if compared with other sub-groups. A few sherds show the evidence of the use of the black slip over the red surface but it is generally washed with black pigment. Sometimes the wash is limited to the rim portion only. Parallel horizontal grooves are also noticed on a few sherds as ornamentation. We notice engraving and graffiti marks also.

C. Wares devoid of slip or wash : These are of medium to thick and coarse fabric. Wares are highly porous with the prominent use of husk and mica. The clay is coarse and less lavigated with generally black core.

Shapes : i. VASES; generally featureless and sharpened rim, carinated near the neck and concave body.

ii. BOWL-cum-lid with clubbed rim and uniformly thickened straight side.

iii. Perforated footed vase.

iv. Storage jars and beakers are suggested by the fragmentary specimens.

N. B. P. Associate : It is made of well lavigated clay by the same potters. The typology and the fabric is also similar to that of the grey ware. The only difference is that it has been fired in oxidizing condition. Therefore the colour of the pot and its section has become red or pinkish instead of greyish or blackish. For the surface treatment red slip is applied.
SHAPES : Dishes and Bowls.

Besides this, coarse red ware associated with N. B. P. ware on the other sites of the Gangetic plain is also noticed. Sherds of this group are of coarse to medium fabric. Red slip is applied for surface treatment. Noticeable shapes are vases decorated with impressed vertical strokes externally and lipped bowls. Miniature vases are also noticed.

Similar pot-sherds were explored from the surface at Banawarighat which lies on upstream of the Manorama river about 8 kms. north west of Gularihavaghat. The other sites in the vicinity are devoid of these painted black and red and painted black slipped wares and contain mostly plain Black Slipped Ware, Grey Ware, N. B. P. Ware and its associated red wares.

Notes

[1] *District Gazetteer of United Province*, Vol. XXXII, 1901, 185.

[2] Ibid, 1.

[3] A. C. L. Carlleyle, *Archaeological Survey of India–A report* Vol. xii.

[4] A. Fuhrer, The Monumental Antiquities and Insciptions in the North-Western Provinces and Oudh, *A. S. I.*, Vol. II, 1891.

[5] P. C. Mukerjee, Antiquities of Kapilvastu, Tarai of Nepal, *A. S. I. R.*, 1901, 43.

[6] Ibid. 43; *D. G. U. P.* Vol. xxxii, 43; Peppe & Smith, *J. R. A. S.*, 1898, 573 ff.

]7] Op. cit. [5].

[8] "About 350 ft. to the north-north-west there is a deep, somewhat circular shaped tank about 120 ft. breadth across called the Hathikund' or the 'Hathigadh', which probably represents the 'Hastigarta' of Buddhist tradition."

Carlleyle, *A. S. I. R*, Vol. xii, 145. But regarding this identification Fuhrer says "The circular tank about 340 ft. to the south of Bhuila Tal still called, according to Mr. Carlleyle, 'Hathikund' was identified by him with the 'Hastigart' of Hiuen-Tsang and General Cunningham is perfectly convinced that this is the spot indicated by in Chinese texts. The *chaukidar* and inhabitants of the neighbouring village state that the name of 'Hathikunda' was given to the tank by Mr. Carlleyle himself and that this name was utterly unknown in that part of country before the arrival of Mr. Carlleyle."

Fuhrer, *A. S. I. R.* Vol. II, 1891, 222.

[9] V. A. Smith, Preparatory Note, Antiquities of Kapilvastu, *A. S. I. R.*, 3–4.

[10] A. C. L. Carlleyle, *Archaeological Survey of India, A Report*, Vol. XII, 113.

[11] Ibid, 189 ff.

[12] A. K. Narain and P. C. Pant, "A Summary Account of Archaeological Exploration in East U. P." *Bharati*, No. 8, Part I, 1964-65.

[13] *Puratattva*, No. 1, 1967-98, 70 ff.

[14] A datailed study of these sherds is to be published elsewhere.

LIST OF SITES IN DISTRICT BASTI

No.	*Name of the Site*	*Tahsil*	*Ceramic Industries*	*Other Finds*	*Previous Reference, if any*	*Remarks*
1.	Agonā	Haraiyā	Red ware	×	×	Circular mound
2.	Bairāgal	do	Red ware	×	×	×
3.	Banawārīghāt	do	Plain & painted Black-&-Red ware; plain & painted Black Slipped ware; Grey ware; NBP, ware; Red ware,	×	×	A chalcolithic site
4.	Bārāhakshetra	do	Red ware,	Structures	Carlleyle, *ASIR*, XII, 211. Fuhrer, *ASI*, II, 1891, 217; A. K. N., *Bharati*, No. 8, part I, p. 120.	×
5.	Bhuilādīh	do	Red ware,	Coins, structures sculptures and T. C. figurines	Carlleyle, *ASIR*, XII, Coins with— (i) Bull and Buddhist symbol; (ii) Sunga and Mitra coins (iii) Kushan coins (iv) Nickle coins (v) Bronze spring ring (vi) Several fragments of sculptures (vii) T. C. figurine of duck and Buddha. pp. 162–171 Fuhrer, *ASI*, II, 1891, 118ff.	Fort walls are still visible, surrounded by ditch and give an idea of a big fortified town.
6.	Gulrihvāghāt	do	Plain & painted Black-&-Red ware; plain & painted Black Slipped ware; Grey ware; NBP. ware and its associate Red ware; Red ware;	Stone and T.C. beads; pottery discs; iron nails; T.C. dabber; perforated cylinder; arrow head; waste flakes	×	A chalcolithic site

7.	*Itawā*	do	Grey ware.	×		Only one sherd of Grey Ware was found as the whole mound is under the construction of a road.
8.	Kopawādīh	do	Red ware.	Structures, brickbats	Carlleyle, *ASIR*, XII, 185. Fuhrer, *ASI*, II, 1891, 221.	×
9.	Makhaurā	do	Red ware.	×	×	Associated with the '*Putresthiyajña*' of king Daśaraṭha.
10.	Pandūrghāt	do	Black Slipped ware; NBP. & its associate wares; Red ware.	×	×	Associated with '*Pāndavas*' crossing the river Manoramā here.
11.	Sabaī	do	Red ware	Structures, brickbats.	×	×
12.	Sringanārī	do	Red ware	×	×	Associated with 'Sringī' Rishi, the chief priest in the Yajña of king Daśaratha.
13.	Ujainiā	do	Red ware, Muslim glazed ware.	×	×	×
14.	Bannī	Bastī	Grey ware; NBP. ware.	Sculpture, T.C. pestles.	×	×
15.	Basahavā	do	Grey ware; NBP. ware; Red ware.	×	×	A stupa suspected.
16.	Bhadanā	do	Red ware.	×	×	×
17.	Bhadeśwaranāth	Bastī	Red ware.	X	X	A modern temple of Śiva

No.	*Name of the Site*	*Tahsil*	*Ceramic Industries*	*Other Finds*	*Previous Reference if any*	*Remarks*
18.	Bhoir	do	Red ware.	X	X	X
19.	Chamarahvāghāt	do	Grey ware, NBP. ware & its associate Red ware.	X	Fuhrer, *ASI*, II, 1891, 224.	X
20.	Devikurhā	do	X	Sculpture	X	A sun image in a modern temple
21.	Gerār	do	Grey ware; NBP. ware & its associates; Red ware. structures;	T.C. pestles; T. C. Potters stamp; T. C. figurines;	X	Suspected to be a big town.
22.	Haradevanāth	do	Grey ware; NBP. and associated Red ware.	T. C. pestles.	X	Modern temple.
23.	Karaūdīh	do	Red ware.	X	Carlleyle, *ASIR*, XII, 217. Fuhrer, *ASI*, II, 1891, 226.	No trace of mound though the village of this name still exists.
24.	Purānīkot	do	Grey ware; NBP. ware & its associates.	×	×	×
25.	Nagar	do	Red ware	×	Carlleyle, *ASIR*, XII, 217; Fuhrer, *ASI*, II, 1891, 225. Cunningham, *Geography of Ancient India*, 350. *Bhāratī*, 8, I, 119.	Suspected to be a big town.

26.	Rāmanagar	do	Grey ware. NBP. and associated Red ware; Red ware.	×	×	×
27.	Sabaīdīh	do	Grey ware; NBP. ware; Red ware.	×	×	×
28.	Tārīpachīsā	do	Grey ware; NBP. ware & its associated wares; Red ware.	Stone bead; T.C. figurines; coins; bone points.	×	Tribal and Kushan coins.
29.	Waraīdīh	do	Red ware.	×	Carlleyle *ASIR*, XII, 220. Fuhrer, *ASI*. II, 1891, 227.	×
30.	Abbāsganj	Khalīlābad	Grey ware; NBP. ware; Red ware.	Coin.	×	Copper cast coin.
31.	Dhauraharā	do	Red ware.	Structures.	×	×
32.	Kopiā	do	Black Slipped ware; Grey ware; Red ware; Muslim-glazed ware.	Coins, thick pot-sherds with glass lump attached.	Fuhrer, *ASI*, II, 1891, 224. *Bhārati*, 8, I, 120.	A fortified town surronnded by ditch; tribal coins.
33.	Magahar	do	Red ware.	Coin.	*Bhārati*, 8. I.119.	Copper cast coin.
34.	Tameswarnāth	do	Red ware.	Coin.	Fuhrer, *ASI*, II, 1891, 226.	Tribal coin, modern temple.
35.	Ujārdīh	Khalīlābad	Black Slipped ware; Grey ware; NBP. ware; Red ware.	Bone points, waste flakes.	×	×
36.	Bhainsā	Bānsī	Red ware.	Coin; structures; T. C. figurine.	*Bhārati*, 8, I, 119.	Kushan coin.
37.	Deokalī	do	Black Slipped ware; NBP. ware; Red Slipped and Red. ware.	T. C. potters impression stamps; structures.	Cunningham, *Geography of Ancient India*, 355.	It seems to be a town having stupa as its contour indicates.

No.	Name of the Site	Tahsil	Ceramic Industries	Other Finds	Previous Reference if any	Remarks
38.	Dharamsinghawā	do	Red ware.	T. C. skin rubber	×	×
39.	Digeswarnāth	do	Red ware.	Carved bricks, sculptures	*Bhārati*; 8, I, 119,	Two ruined temples.
40.	Fulawariā	do	Red ware.	T. C. spout; sculpture.	×	Siva image having three mouths, front facing to the east, locally called '*Bhavāni Sankar*'.
41.	Gosfāri	do	Red ware; Muslim glazed ware.	T. C. figurine.	*Bhārati* 8, I, 119.	×
42.	Paunā	do	Black Slipped ware; Grey ware; Red ware.	×	×	×
43.	Piparpatiā	do	Grey ware; NBP. & associated Red ware; Red ware.	Waste flakes, bead making rod.	×	×
44.	Purainā	do	Grey ware; Red ware.	T. C. pestles.	×	×
45.	Tharaulī	do	Black Slipped ware; Grey ware; NBP. ware; Red ware.	T. C. pestles, structures.	×	×
46.	Awainiā	Domariāganj	Black Slipped ware; Grey ware; NBP. ware; Red ware.	Structures.	×	Half portion of the mound is inhabited by present people.
47.	Bhāratbhārī	do	Red ware.	Structures; T. C. figurines.	Fuhrer, *ASI*, 1891, 223.	Suspected to be a big city.
48.	Buddhīkhās	do	Grey ware; NBP. ware; Red ware.	×	×	Mound is occupied by present people.

49.	Chaisāre	do	Black Slipped ware; NBP. ware; Red ware.	T. C. beads, structures	×	×
50.	Dhauraharā	do	Red ware.	×	×	×
51.	Gālāpār	do	Red ware.	T. C. animal figurine.	×	Forestified area.
52.	Hansuṇī	do	Red ware.	T. C. human figurine, structures	×	×
53.	Jiganā	do	Red ware.	×	×	Modern temple.
54.	Kateśwarnāth	do	×	×	×	A Modern temple associated with Kuśa, son of king Rāma, and previously this place was known as Kuśeswarnāth.
55.	Kaṭhelā	Domariāganj	Red ware	Sculptures	Fuhrer, *ASI*, II, 1891, 223.	Suspected to be a big town.
56.	Kesār	do	Red ware.	Carved bricks piled in the plinth of a modern house.	×	×
57.	Kopā	do	Red ware.	T. C. human figurines; structures.	×	A town suspected.
58.	Nakhtardeoriā	do	Red ware.	Ink-pot type lid.	×	×
59.	Perārī	do	Red ware.	×	Fuhrer, *ASI*, II, 1891.	×
60.	Sarpokā	do	Red ware.	T. C. Pestle, pottery disc.	×	Mound is under construction of tubewell and drains forirrigation.

No.	*Name of the Site*	*Tahsīl*	*Ceramic Industries*	*Other Finds*	*Previous Reference, if any*	*Remarks*
61.	Tenuhār	do	Black Slipped ware; Grey ware; NBP. ware; Red ware.	T. C. potters stamp, ink-pot type lid, handmade human figurines, structures.	×	Suspected to be a big town.
62.	Karamā	Naugarh	Grey ware; NBP. ware. Red ware.	T. C. figurines and coins are reported by local people.	×	Suspected to be a stupa.
63.	Genewariā	do	Grey ware; NBP. ware; Red ware.	Iron ring, structures.	×	Suspected to be a small fort.
64.	Malapār orNanakār	do	Red ware.	×	×	×
65.	Pīparāhwā	do	Grey ware; NBP. ware, Red ware.	×	*JRAS*, 1898, 573 ff.	Stupa, Dr. N. R. Banerjee believes it to be ancient 'Kapilavastu'.
66.	Piparī	do	×	×	×	Seventeen small stupas are still visible.
67.	Soharatgarh	do	Red ware.	T. C. pestles, structures.	×	×

A study in the Stone Age of Khajuraho[1] in Central India

by KRISHNA KUMAR

INTRODUCTION

Renowned for the temples of the Chandella Period (10th-12th centuries A. D.), Khajurāho is otherwise unknown as a habitat of the prehistoric man. In the past, several Stone Age sites [2] were discovered in the valleys of River Ken and its tributaries, but the basin of River Khūdar—another branch of the former, where Khajurāho is situated—had attracted scant attention of the prehistorians [3]. The author explored the central region of the

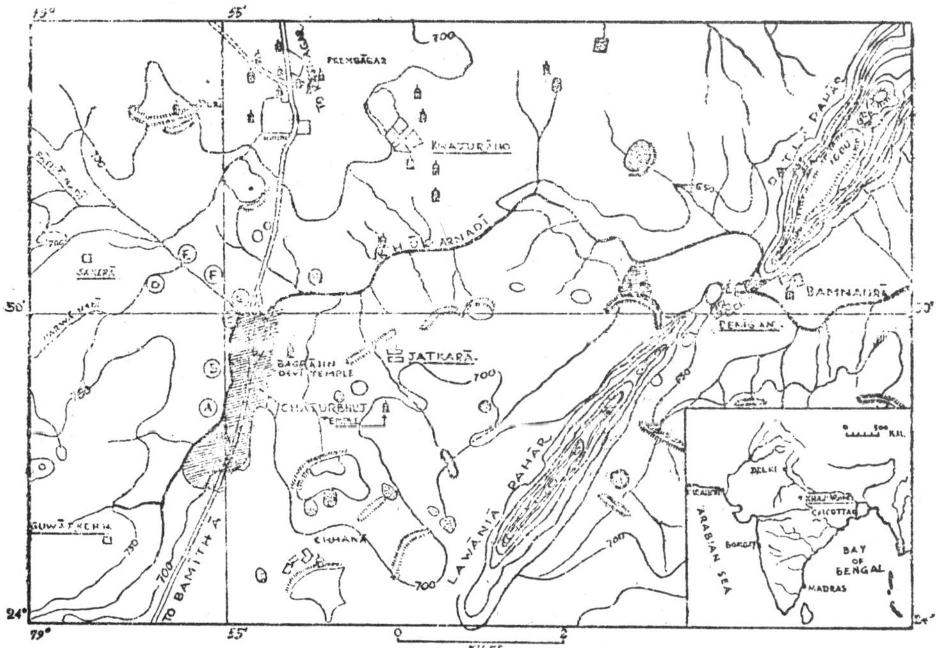

REFERENCES:- FACTORY SITES OTHER LOCALITIES (A)

Fig. 1

valley of River Khūdar during the period between 1961 64, and located two open-air factory sites and eight other localities [4] yielding artefacts of the Middle Stone Age [5], Late Stone Age and neolithic industries. The object of this paper is to report these discoveries and to bring home their significance in the light of available evidence.

THE SITES AND THEIR LOCATION

Within a radius of 4 km. from village Khajurāho (Lat. 24° 51′ N.--Long. 80° 0′ E.) District Chhatarpur, Madhya Pradesh, are located ten Stone Age sites, on either bank of the River Khūdar and its affluents (fig 1). Of these, the two extensive factory sites lie within the revenue jurisdictions of villages Jaṭkarā and Benīgunj, and the rest (No A to H) are located near Guārkachha, Sakerā, Khajurāho and Benīgunj.

The factory site situated on the Rājnagar-Bamīṭhā Road, at a distance of about 1 km. west of village Jaṭkarā, is the most extensive in this area. Located as it is on the right bank of the River Khūdar (opposite to its junction with the Pāṭhā Nālā), the two fords [6] connect it with the other localities (No. A to G) situated respectively, on its north and west. It is dotted with a number of gneissic outcrops [7], in which microliths are found in abundance. As the site covers the cremation ground, it was found littered with the pot-sherds (ordinary red ware) of modern period.

The other factory site, though much smaller in area, is also located near a ford which connects villages Benīgunj and Bamnaurā—situated on opposite banks of the river. Locality No. H, lying over a *nullāh* beyond Lawānia Pahar, indicates the eastward extension of the chain of Stone Age sites.

TOPOGRAPHY

The low-lying central tract around Khajurāho, where the Stone Age sites are located, is a level and often a stone-hewn plain. While the entire northern and western region is dotted with the masses of irregularly heaped boulders of gneiss, the area on its southern and eastern fringes is flanked by the cliffs of overlying Vindhyans. The valley in the central tract is drained by the system of a non-perennial stream—Khūdar Nadī, which flowing in south-west-north-easterly direction cuts deep gorges through the Vindhyan outliers and divides one of them into a pair of segments, known as Datlā and Lawāniā Pahār, respectively. With a height of 1,000 feet (about 305 m.) from sea-level, the former is the highest range of the area. With shallow channels, the flat banks of this river-system are covered with the flood alluvium. Except some cultivated fields, the whole tract is sparsely covered with jungle.

Located over or near the gneissic outcrops in the central tract, all the Stone Age sites overlook the river or one of its affluents. "These small rocky eminences, now usually bare of cultivation, having a good all round view, are the favourite sites on which mesolithic hunters must have had their groups of huts" [8]. Probably it is due to the physical semi-isolation of the area, that the lithic industries of this area show a curious pattern of survival and progress.

GEOLOGY

Corresponding to its three-fold physical division, the area is geologically too, divisible into three regions. The central tract, where Khajurāho with its Stone Age sites is situated, is more or less a plain with outcrops of the gneiss and other allied rocks. The north-western part is characterised by the Archaeans of Bundelkhand—a pink variety of granites—which is often relieved by low steep hills of quartz reef and numerous dikes and sills of black-basalt (Deccan Trap) cut through the gneiss. The geodes of the Deccan Trap contain varieties of agate, carnelian, opal, onyx, jasper, etc. The south eastern section lying in the Pannā Range of the Vindhyans, show the Lower Vindhyan Strata with outcrops of the Bijāwars at their base and occasionally also having the Kaimūr sandstones. While these formations are rich in variegated siliceous material like chalcedony, chert and agate, the most characteristic rocks of the Bijāwars are the layers of banded jasper of red colour, which are frequently intercalated amidst limestones and due to its highly ferruginious nature they are also found impregnated with the haematite concretions. These geological formations were probably the source of raw-material for the various lithic industries of this area.

A dry stony red earth, known as *rānkar*, is the commonest soil in the gneissic area and the hills, which generally speaking is less fertile. Of other soils, *kābar*, *parwā*, and *motā* (*mār*) deserve mention; while the first two are light soils, the last one is an inferior variety of the black cotton soil and met with only in the intrusive dikes of the trap-rock. Lastly, a thin layer of the alluvium has been deposited by the river on its flood-plain. The general poverty of the soil and the low rain-fall were perhaps among some of the factors responsible for the economic backwardness and cultural stagnation of the prehistoric Khajurāho.

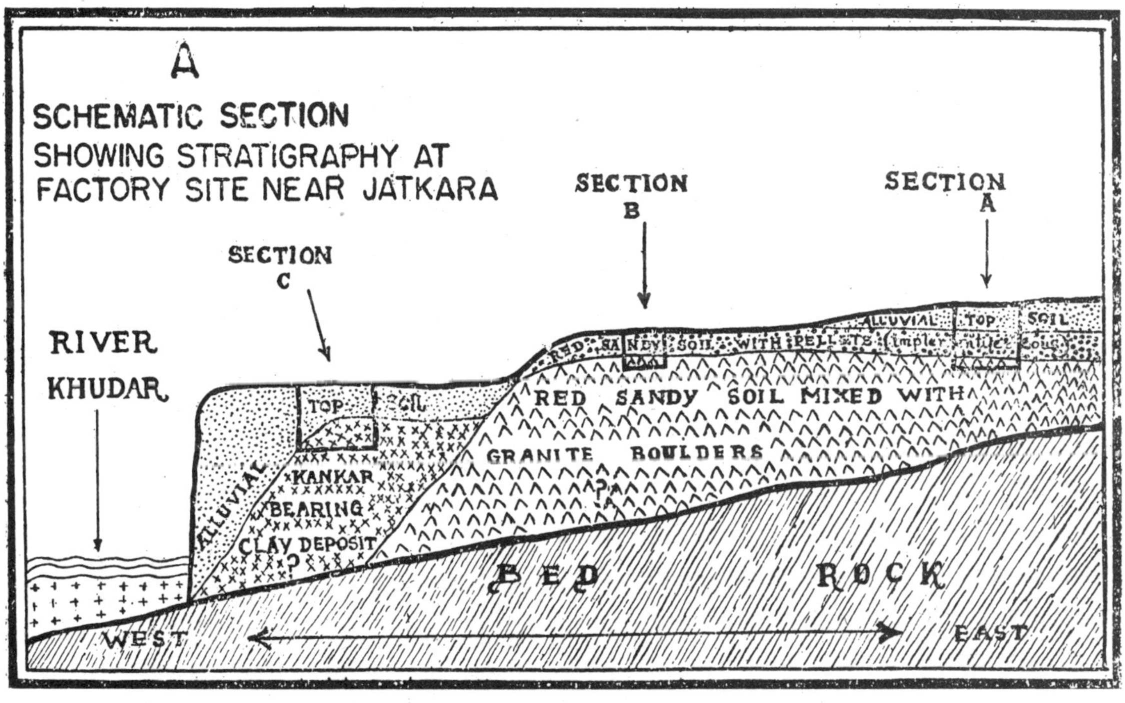

Fig. 2

STRATIGRAPHY

In absence of cliff-sections at any of the sites, it is difficult to make a correct appraisal of the stratigraphic position of different lithic industries in relation to various geological deposits. but an idea, though vague, may be formed on the basis of three small sections (fig. 2) noticed at the factory site near Jaṭkarā and described below :—

I. A recent road-section (Section A) at a high level, near the Bagrājin Devī Temple, [8 a] shows that a 18 to 48 cm. thick implementiferous deposit made of red sandy soil (hard *murum*) mixed up with stone pellets is underlain by a thick deposit of red sandy soil and granite boulders which finally rests over the gneissic bed-rock. Whereas the upper layer has yielded artefacts of the microlithic assemblage, the lower deposit does not yield any tool. The implementiferous deposit, in turn, is finally sealed by another 18 to 48 cm. thick layer of flood loam. Numerous flakes and nodules of basalt together with the haematite pebbles were gathered from the surface.

II. At a lower level, near the stream, where the top alluvial soil is subject to erosion due to the flow of rain-water and cultivation, the implementiferous red sandy soil was found exposed showing a few clusters of the microliths, which probably mark the spots of different workshops, where these tools were manufactured [9]. The Middle Stone Age artefacts and the neoliths were found loose on its surface. In a small pit (Section B), it was observed that the 41 cm. thick implementiferous layer is underlain by a red sandy soil deposit of unknown thickness, but the former did not yield any artefact other than the microliths.

III. Another section (Section C), situated at a still lower level, near the river bank, consists of a *kaṅkar* bearing clay deposit of unknown thickness, sealed by a 64 cm. to 1·86 m. thick deposit of the alluvial soil. Although no tool was encountered in the kankary deposit, a number of microliths and neoliths, together with a small fragment of bone and a broken bead (fig. 6, A) were recovered from the surface of the alluvium.

From the foregoing description, it may be concluded that whereas the microlithic industry is contained in the implementiferous red sandy soil, the artefacts of the Middle Stone Age and the neoliths occur on the surface.

The Middle Stone Age Industry

It is essentially a flake-blade-scraper assemblage popularly known as 'Series II'-industry.

With the exception of a few flakes and four implements obtained from the factory site near Benīgunj, rest of the surface-collection comprising twenty tools and numerous akes was solely made at the factory site near Jaṭkarā and a solitary convex scraper on pebble was picked up from the adjoining river-bed near Khūdar Bridge.

Since none of them was recovered from any of the geological deposits *in situ* and a few of them are slightly rolled or abrased, they may be taken to have been transported by the river from elsewhere, but in view of the freshness of most of the tools, the shallow river banks and the considerably damaged land surface at both the factory sites (due to the part played by various natural and human agencies), they appear to have been manufactured there itself. However, so far as the stratigraphic position of this industry is concerned, it has yet to be determined by a trial excavation at the site near Jaṭkarā as well as an intensive exploration in the upper and the lower reaches of the stream.

The artefacts are made on different fine grained rocks, but the majority of them are on chert. Though most of the flakes and implements have obtuse angled striking platform and unworked undersurface, the occurrence of round oval flakes with prepared platform and previous work before their detachment from cores, betrays the employment of the Levallois technique. As there are some parallel sided blades together with two fluted cores and a few tools are made on short, thick and parallel sided flakes, it indicates the knowledge of the flake-blade technique. While certain tools bear flutings or marginal retouch by wood hammer technique, others show a tenon or notch for hafting and also some efforts at blunting the backs and sides for easy handling. Sometimes they are so demunitive in size that they almost merge with the tools of the microlithic (Late Stone Age) industry, which appears to have evolved from the former. They are stained red due to their cccurrence on the red sandy soil.

Besides other artefacts characterstic of this industry, viz., various flakes, blades, scrapers, borers, a point, and two fluted cores, it also includes the unfinished specimens of a big pebble chopper [10] and a small handaxe [11]. Although the two doubtful finds are not of much archaeological value, they together with a small pebble scraper probably indicate survival of the Early Stone Age tradition in the succeeding stage. A close scrutiny of certain tools, particularly blades and fluted cores, testifies its advanced character, and reminds us of the Upper Palaeolithic facies of Europe. Some of the artefacts even show the patination marks of orange or dark colour in varying degrees. Typologically this industry seems to represent a purely food gathering economy, based on hunting.

The artefacts of this industry, are comparable to the Middle and Upper Palaeolithic tools reported from different parts of Bundelkhaṇḍ [12] and elsewhere in India [13].

The Microlithic Industry

It is a mixed assemblage of the non-geometric and the geometric microliths of the Late Stone Age tradition together with an over-all majority of the short parallel sided blades.

As it profusely occurs in stratified deposit of the implementiferous red sandy soil at all the sites, it is perhaps the most prolific industry of Khajurāho.

Though it is manufactured on varieties of crypto-crystalline colloidal silica and rarely on quartz or trap, like many other microlithic industries of Bundelkhaṇḍ & Baghelkhand, it is essentially made on chert and chalcedony.

Besides the use of free flaking punch technique, this industry also shows the application of 'crested-guiding-ridge' technique in the preparation of short parallel sided blades. In addition to the tenons and notches intentionally provided for hafting, the artefacts bear secondary work by nibbling, oblique, steep and ridge-back retouch.

Probably owing to the small size of the available raw material, the blade industry of Khajurāho primarily consists of short and narrow parallel sided flakes (ribbon flakes) and is accompanied by a few backed blades, crescents and lunates with long chords, trapezes, triangles, arrowheads, points and scrapers on parallel sided flakes together with a number of various blades, points, scrapers, borers and burins, on assymetrical flakes as well as some scrapers, borers, points and burins ingeneously manufactured on exhausted fluted cores, their flakes and the broken tools.

The two factory sites abound in sharp and pointed flakes which in the absence of retouch can not be defined as 'microliths', in true sense, but they could have definitely served the simple needs of the prehistoric man; this fact is amply witnessed by the occurrence of a large number of used flakes.

Since the relative stratigraphic position of the Late Stone Age and ribbon-flake elements of this microlithic assemblage is not known, it may tentatively be taken to represent a mixed economy of the transitional (proto-neolithic) stage when the people had already switched over to the methods of 'subsistence agriculture', but in order to increase their food supply, they still resorted, to a large extent, to the old practice of hunting and fishing. It is also likely that though Khajurāho

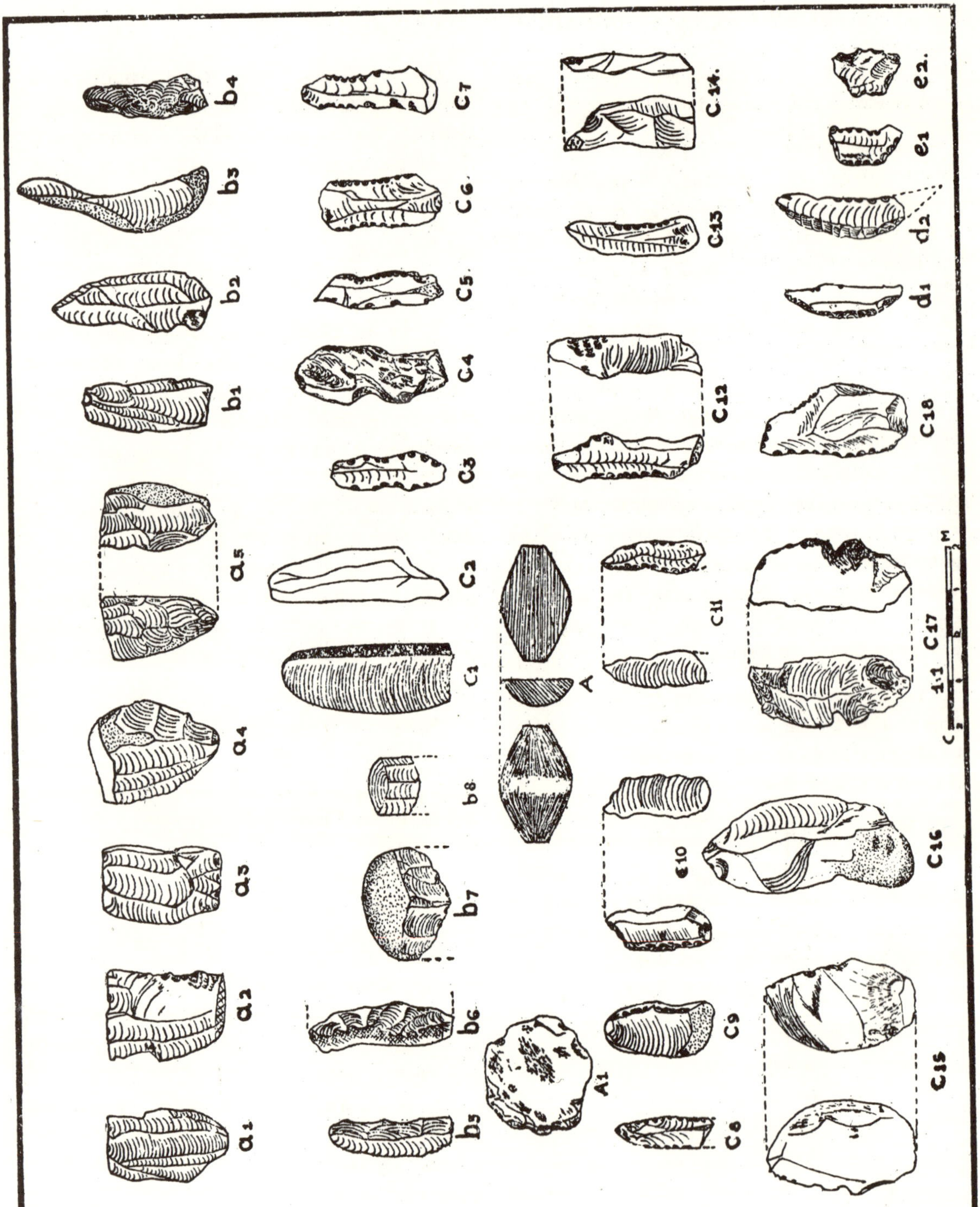

Fig. 3

was largely in the food gathering stage, still the Short Blade Industry flourished there mainly to meet the demands of the Neolithic-Chalcolithic village communities settled along the arterial rivers, in the neighbourhood where copper being a rare and costly material [14] its use was substituted by the ribbon-flake tools.

Whereas similar mixed microlithic assemblage of urban and hunting types have been reported from Tripurī, [15] Chhoṭā Simlā (Jabalpur), Pachmarhī, etc., [16] in Central India and Karāchī District in Sind[17], most of the artefacts of this industry are techno-typologically comparable with the lithic remains found in the Neolithic-Chalcolithic levels at different sites in Central and Western India.

Not taking into consideration the multitudinous ordinary cores, various dressing flakes, as well as numerous used flakes and semi-finished tools, the artefacts of this industry my be classified into following types and sub-types :-

I. *Cores* :—(i) Short fluted cores with pointed end, 107 (fig. 3, a1); (ii) with oblique end, 14 (fig. 3, a2); (iii) with flat base, 4 (fig. 3, a 3); (iv) showing cross-flaking, 19 (fig. 3, a4); (v) with crested-guiding-ridge, 1 (fig. 3, a 5); and (vi) partly flaked, 10 (not illustrated).

II. *Flakes* :—(i) short and narrow parallel sided flakes, 437 (fi. 3, b1); (ii) with pointed end, 173 (fig. 3, b2); (iii) plunging flakes, 20 (fig. 3, b3); (iv) crested-guiding-flakes, 9 (fig. 3, b4); (v) secondary guiding flakes, 24 (fig. 3, b5); (vi) spur removing flakes, 2 (fig. 3, b6); and (vii) core-rejuvenation flakes, 11 (fig. 3, b7 & 8).

III. *Blades* :—(i) short and narrow single straight sided blades with single or double ridge, natural back and with or without a tenon, 9 (fig. 3, c1 & 2); (ii) with partly or fully blunted back, 36 (fig. 3, c3); (iii) with notched edge, 3 (fig. 3, c4); (iv) with pointed end, 12 (fig. 3, c5); (v) short and narrow double straight sided blades with uni-or bi-marginally retouched edge, 37 (fig. 3, c6); (vi) with serrated edge, 6 (fig. 3, c7); (vii) with pointed end, 1 (fig. 3, c1); (viii) pen knife blades with round, angular or pointed end, 17 (fig. 3, c9-11); (ix) parallel sided blade-*cum*-side scrapers, 3 (fig. 3, c12); (x) parallel sided pointed blade-*cum*-side scrapers, 2 (fig. 3, c13); (xi) parallel sided blade-*cum*-borer, 1 (fig. 3, c14) (xii) ordinary blades with natural back and use marks on edge. 5 (fig. 3, c15); (xiii) with double edge a d a tenon, 1 (fig. 3, c16); (xiv) with single edge, tenon and notch, 1 (fig. 3, c17); and (xv) with pointed end, 1 (fig. 3, c18).

IV. *Lunates* :—(i) with ridge on dorsal surface, 21 (fig. 3, dl), and (ii) without ridge, 11 (fig. 3, d2).

V. *Trapezes* :—(i) with two oblique sides and the back blunted by steep retouch and use marks on the edge, 1 (fig. 3, e1); and (ii) with oblique retouch on the three sides and serrated edge, 1 (fig. 3, e2).

VI. *Trapezoids* :—(i) with three sides blunted and use marks on the edge, 1 (fig. 4, a1); and (ii) with one or two sides blunted and use marks on the edge, 3 (fig. 4, a2).

VII. *Triangles* :—(i) scalene, 22 (fig. 4, b1 ; (ii) isocele, 6 (fig. 4, b2); and (iii) scalene made on a thick ordinary quartz flake, 1 (fig. 4, b3).

VIII. *Points* :—(i) leaf shaped points with a blunted or unblunted thick side and without a notch or tang, 25 (fig. 4, c1&2); (ii) with uni-marginal retouch and with or without a notch

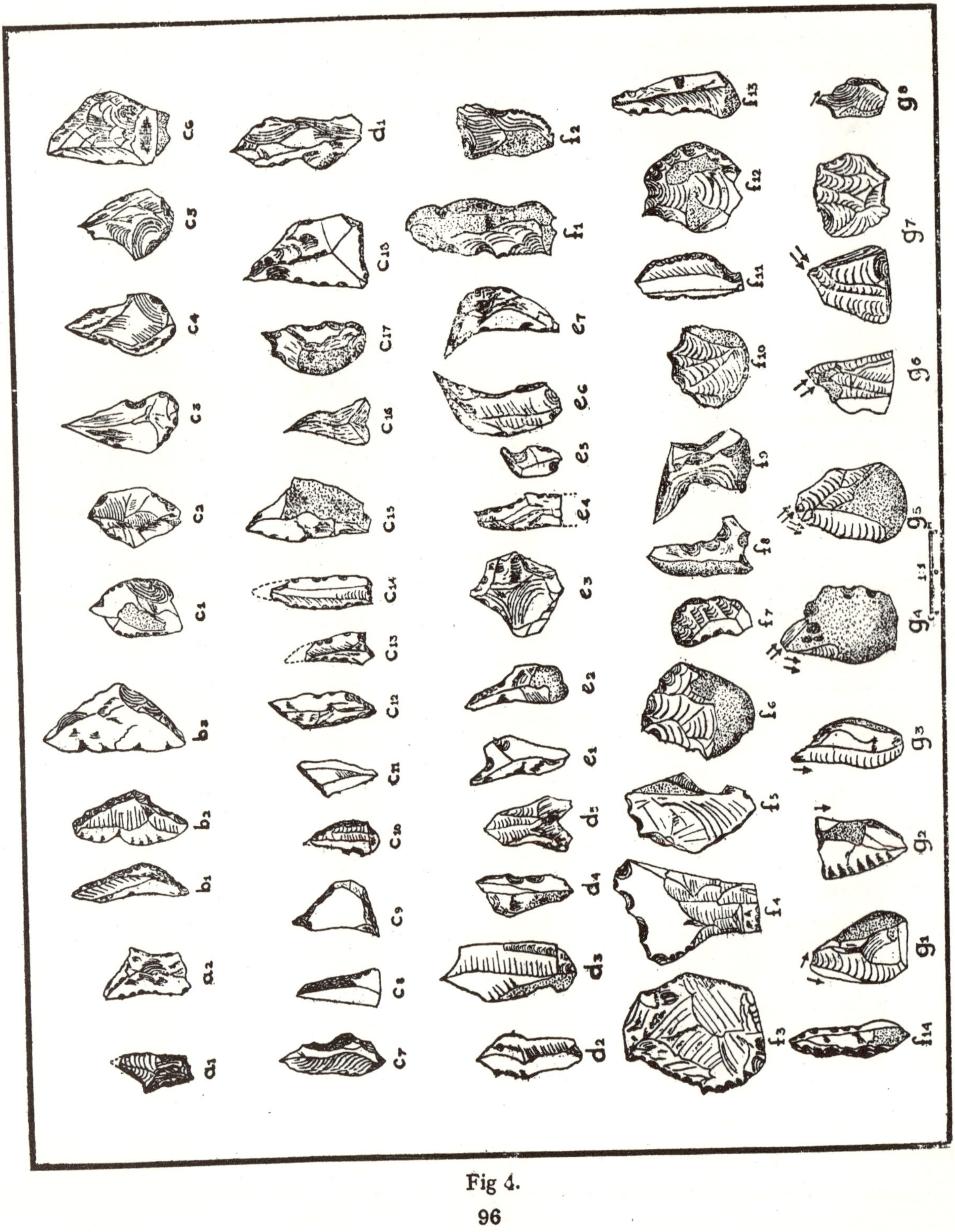

Fig 4.

or tang or with both, 19 (fig. 4, c3); (iii) similar to above but with bi-marginal retouch, 48 (fig. 4, c4 & 5); (iv) similar to above but showing pressure flaking in the centre of the dorsal side, bi-marginal retouch and a tenon, 1 (fig. 4, c6); v) crescentic points with partly or fully blunted arch, 21 (fig. 4, c7 & 8); (vi) with bulging back, 2 (fiig. 4, c9); (vii) with blunted arch and retouched chord, 8 (fig. 4, c 10); (viii) obliquely blunted points, 6 (fig. 4, c11); (ix) pen knife points, 1 (fig. 4, c12); (x) asymmetric hollow based points, 3, (fig.4,c13); (xi) symmetric hollow based points, 5 (fig.4, c14); (xii) beaked points, 15 (fig. 4, c15 & 16); (xiii) beaked point-*cum*-side scraper, 15 (fig 4, c17), and (xiv) beaked point-*cum*-end scraper, 1 (fig. 4, c18).

IX. *Arrow-heads*:—(i) with single shouldered tang, 6 (fig.4, d1); (ii) with double shouldered tang, 5 (fig.4, d2); (iii) with parallel sided tang, 9 (fig. 4, d3); (iv) oblique arrow heads with uni-marginally retouched tang, (fig. 4, d4); and (v) with double antenna, 3 (fig. 4,d5) [18].

X. *Borers* :—(i) with uni-marginally retouched short or long end, 17 (fig. 4, e1 & 2); (ii) with bi-marginal retouch, 12 (fig. 4,e3): (iii) drill with bi-marginally retouched long borer end, 1 (fig. 4, e4); (iv) beaked borers, 3 (fig.4, e5); (v) beaked borer-*cum*-concave scrapers, 2 (fig. 4, e6); and (vi) beaked borer-*cum*-convex scraper, 1 (fig. 4. e7).

XI. *Scrapers* :—(i) Side scrapers, 60 (fig. 4, f1); (ii) side *cum*-end scrapers, 15 (fig.4, f2); (iii) side scraper-*cum* borers, 4 (fig. 4, f3); (iv) end scrapers, 22 (fig.4, f4); (v) end scraper with uni-marginally blunted tang, 1 (fig. 4, f5); (vi) end scraper-*cum*-borer, 1 (fig.4, f6); (vii) end-*cum*-concavo-convex scraper, 1 (fig. 4, f7): (viii) concave scrapers, 9 (fig. 4, f8); (ix) concave scraper-*cum*-borers, 20 (fig. 4, f9); (x) core-scrapers, 20 (fig.4,f10) (xi) convex scraper, 15 (fig.4, f11) (xii) convex scraper-*cum*-borers , 5 (fig. 4, f12); and (xiii) parallel sided scraper-*cum*-borers, 5 (fig. 4, f13 & 14) [19].

XII. *Burins* :—(i) with a vertical spall against a transverse spall, 1 (fig.4, g1); (ii) with a vertical spall against a steep retouch; a burin-*cum*-side scraper, 1 (fig.4 g 2); (iii) with a vertical spall against steep retouch, 1 (fig. 4, g3); (iv) with a set of two oblique spalls on either side, 2 (fig. 4, g4 & 5); (v) with a set of two small oblique spalls on one side, 1 (fig. 4, g6); and (vi) a burin-*cum*-convex scraper, 1 (fig. 4, g7).

XIII. *Micro-burin* ;—is represented by a single specimen in the collection (fig.4, g8).

XIV. *Bead* :— A damaged barrel-shaped bead on banded agate, but showing no perforation (fig. 3, A) [19 a].

THE NEOLITHIC INDUSTRY

It is a ground stone axe industry represented by a surface-collection consisting of numerous flakes and nodules together with about a dozen implements in the various stages of production.

Whereas the trap flakes and nodules were gathered from different sites, the tool collection was solely made at the factory site near Jaṭkarā.

Excluding mace-heads made on granite and sandstone, rest of the artefacts are on dike-basalt.

Although flaking, pecking and grinding are the techniques which have commonly been employed in the preparation of tools, it appears as if the method of polishing has sparingly been used to finish the working edges of the axes only. A few of the tools successfully

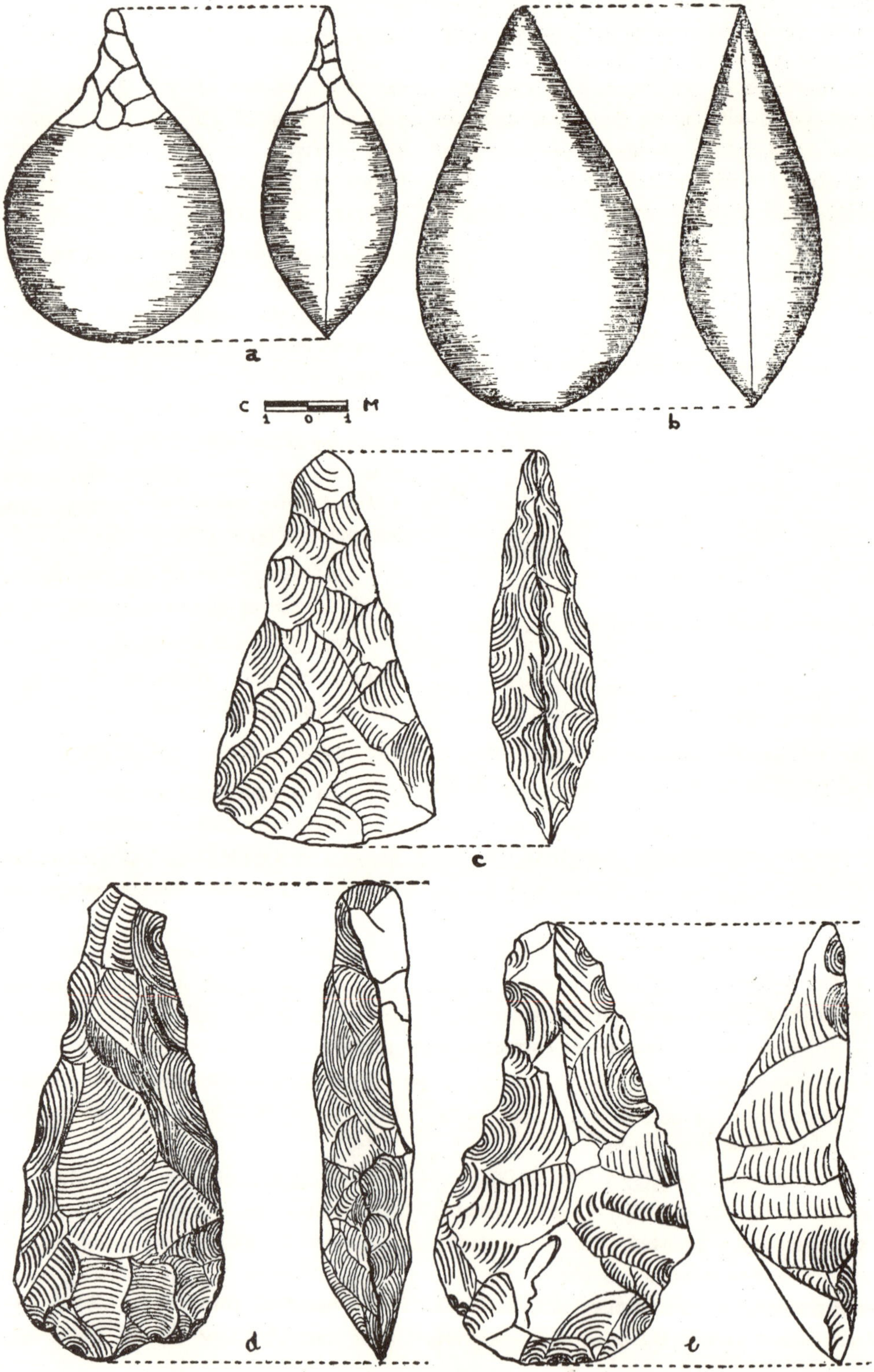

Fig. 5

manufactured with minimum work, on oblong multi plane nodules of trappoid rock, look almost as naturally shaped artefacts. The battered butts and damaged edges of the axes and the adzes; and the broken mace heads and sling balls are presumably due to their frequent hafting and heavy use. The artefacts bear orange coloured marks of patination, in varying degrees.

Besides the casual surface finds from different parts of Bundelkhaṇḍ and Baghelkhaṇḍ, [20] neolithic celts have also been obtained from the upper level of the neolithic-chalcolithic phase at Eraṇ, [21] in central India. The neolithic tools of Khajurāho are comparable with those found at Brahmagirī, [22] Saṅgankallū, [23] Piklīhāl, [24] Nāgārjunakoṇḍā, [25] Tekkalkoṭā [26] etc. in south and different sites in central and eastern India [27].

The typological description of the limited material is given below :—

I. *Axes* :—(i) Showing lenticular cross-section and pointed butt-end, it has a marginally polished edge; with extensively battered butt, it is the smallest but most finished tool in the collection (fig. 5, a). (ii) Similar to above but without any polish (fig. 5, b). (iii) Showing a rough quadrilateral cross-section and an irregular edge, it is an unfinished specimen with alternately flaked surface (fig. 5, c). (iv) With bifacially flaked straight edge and round butt-end, it could have also been used as a wedge (not illustrated). (v) A fragment of a polished axe with straight cutting edge (not illustrated).

II. *Adze* :—Showing a triangular cross-section and longitudinally bent body, it has a broad, steeply bevelled convex edge and a tongue-like end. A notch on the left margin

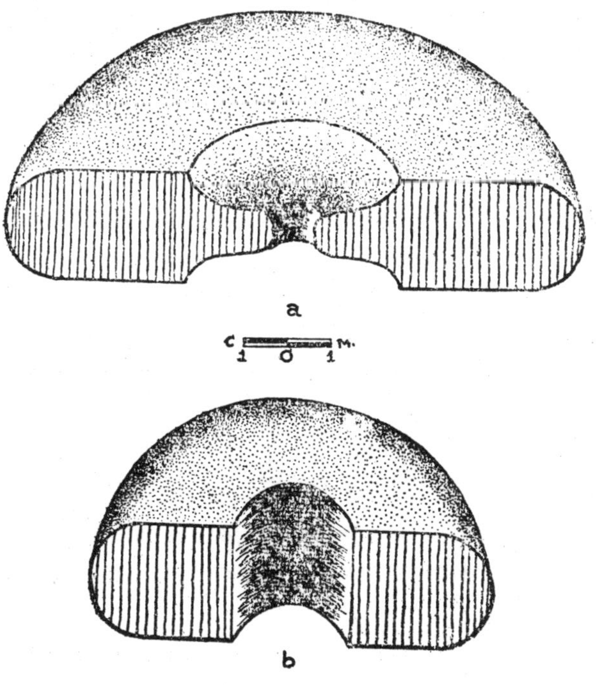

Fig. 6

of dorsal side indicates that it was probably hafted in the middle at right angle to the handle. With smooth natural surface on either side and unpolished body, it is a semi-finished artefact. (fig. 5, e).

III. *Hoes* :–[28] (i) With trapezoidal cross-section, steeply bevelled narrow edge and oblique butt-end, it is a typical specimen of an almost naturally shaped tool, flaked only on the flat ventral surface and left margin of the dorsal side with a little grinding on the dorsal edge, probably due to its constant use as a hoe [29].

(ii) With an almost trapezoidal cross-section, flat butt-end and thoroughly flaked body, it is an unfinished but the biggest piece in the collection (fig. 5, d) [30].

IV. *Mace-heads* :—(i) A broken piece on sandstone, showing incomplete hour-glass section with cup-like lateral depressions, worked from both the faces and ground surface (fig. 6, a). (ii) Another broken piece on granite; it is similar to above, but for the lateral depressions (fig. 6, b).

V. *Sling-balls* :—Two fragments of small spheroids, about an inch in diameter (not illustrated).

VI. *Stone-vase*:—A fragment of the rim of a vase or bowl trap, obtained from Locality G.

CHRONOLOGY

Since the stratigraphic position of the Middle Stone Age artefacts is unknown, they cannot be dated in absolute terms, however, in view of their advanced character (the presence of Upper Palaeolithic element), they may be ascribed to the transitional phase of the Middle and Late Stone Age. Contained as it is in a recent geological horizon the implementiferous red sandy soil deposit sealed by a modern flood layer the microlithic industry must have flourished in early middle Holocene. Although it is a mixed assemblage and no habitation site yielding ribbon-flake tools in association of painted pottery and copper–the two essential attributes of the Neolithic-Chalcolithic culture–has so far been discovered in this area [32], still the predominance of the short parallel sided flakes over other microliths; the persence of numerous short fluted cores together with a few crested-guiding flakes; the survival of a few backed blades, lunates and crescents with long chord and trapezes; and lastly the occurrence of neoliths on the surface of the implementiferous deposit containing the microlithic industry, are among the facts which point towards the possible symbiotic relationship of the microlithic and neolithic industries of Khajurāho with the Neolithic-Chalcolithic complex of central and western India, which as a result of the latest Carbon-14 dating has been placed within a date bracket of *circa* 2000-1000 B. C. [33]. with a possibility of extension of the upper limit as late as 7th. century B. C. [34].

Since the neolithic industry does not occur in any geological context and the artefacts were found un-associated with and scattered over a greater area than those of other industries, they appear to be posterior [35] to the microlithic industry and thus mark the last phase of the Stone Age human activities at Khajurāho.

CONCLUSIONS

Since the material obtained as a result of the surface-collection is neither in plenty nor stratified, the conclusions deduced in the foregoing pages are tentative and need confirmation by an intensive field-work in this area. However, besides placing Khajurāho and its environs on the prehistoric map of India, the present discoveries have also broadly indicated that, like other parts of this sub-continent, this area too, though in a slow pace, passed through most of the major phases [36] of human technological evolution in the Stone Age. As a result, the antiquity of Khajurāho generally held to be beginning only with the mediaeval period has now been pushed back to a remote past. It has also clearly shown that the peninsular neolithic culture had a very wide distribution which besides encompassing the Deccan and the Mālwā Plateaux, [37] also flourished in central India, and was not only confined to the south-east as hitherto thought by worman [38], Dani [39] and others [40]. A neolithic province for the central and western India has already been proposed by Krishnaswami. [41] , but as Thapar [42] has rightly pointed out, there is absence of a sharp distinction between the neolithic and the chalcolithic cultural stages manifested in these assemblages. As the transition between food-collecting and food-producing was perhaps a very short-lived phenomenon in this region, on the other hand, it has also been suggested by Mohapatra [43] that some of the non-geometric microlithic industries with pottery are neolithic rather than mesolithic. However, if Khajurāho and other sites in Bundelkhaṇḍ and Baghelkhaṇḍ regions yielding the microlithic and neolithic industries are thoroughly investigated, it is likely that we may get definite evidences of the pure neolithic culture in stratified context there also and thus the existing gap between the southern and the eastern neolithic provinces will be filled up by the central Indian neolithic province.

Though the picture that has emerged out of the work is nebulous, yet, if the large tract around Khajurāho, including the valleys of rivers Urmil and Kuṭnī–the two other tributaries of river Ken,—which still lies uninvestigated, is subjected to an intensive field work, it would not only reveal the pattern of the distribution of different lithic industries in this area, but may also focus new light on various problems concerning the stone age studies of this egion, namely, the geological formations and their correlation with the climatic changes of the Quaternary; the stratigraphic position of the Middle Stone Age artefacts and the associated Upper Palaeolithic element; the relative stratigraphic position if any) of the various components of the microlithic assemblage; the possible association of painted pottery and copper with the parallel-sided blade tools and their relation with the overlying neoliths; the existence or otherwise of rock-shelters in the surrounding hills, and yield other cultural and environmental data [44] as well; and thus a concrete image of the prehistoric Khajurāho will stand unveiled.

With the completion of the Benī Sāgar Dam, the vast land stretch lying within its catchment area will go under water. It would be in the interest of the prehistoric research, if the area is explored prior to the submergence.

Acknowledgements

The author wishes to express his deep sense of indebtedness to Professor (Dr.) H. D. Sankalia, Dr. V. N. Mishra, Dr. Z. D. Ansari and Shri S. N. Rajguru of the Deccan College, Poona, for so generously extending their help and guidance in the study of this collection, during his stay at their institute. He is deeply beholden to Shri M. N. Deshpande and Shri B. K. Thapar, respectively Joint Director General and Director (Explorotions), Archaeological Survey of India, New Delhi, and Shri P. C. Pant of the Banaras Hindu University, who were kind enough to offer their valuable suggestions. His grateful thanks are also due to Shri S. R. Rao and Dr. N R. Banerjee, the then Superintendents, Archaeological Survey of India, Agra, as it was due to their encouragements that he could do this field work. Lastly, but not the least, he is obliged to Shri V. Thomas Chandy, Surveyor, Archaeologica Survey of India, Varanasi, for kindly taking all pains in prepartion of the map of the area and the line-drawings of the stone implements illustrated here, and also to Shri S. K. Kapoor, who kindly typed the script.

Notes

[1] Originally submitted in a briefer form to the fifty-fifth session of the Indian Science Congress, Varanasi, (January, 1968).

[2] *Indian Archaeology 1957-58 ' A Aeview*, 25-26; *Ibid.*, 1958-59, 26 & 72; B. Allchin, 'The Indian Middle Stone Age', *Bulletin of Institute of Archaeology*, No. II, (London, 1959), 1 ff; R. V. Joshi, 'The Stone Age industries of Damoh Area', *Ancient India*, No. 17, (1961), 5 ff, P. C. Pant, 'Some Lithic Tool Industries of Banda', *Bharati : Bulletin of the College of Indology*, (B. H. U.), No. 7, pt. I & II, (Varanasi, 1963-64), 114 ff.

[3] J. Coggin Brown, *Catalogue ofP reshistoric Antiquities in the Indian Museum*, (Simla, 1917), 85; *Indian Archaeology*, 1961-62 *A Review*, 94.

[4] H. D. Sankalia, 'Fresh Look at Khajuraho', *Times of India*, (April, 10, 1966), 8; Sankalia, 'Socio-Economic and Geographical Background of Khajuraho', *Journal of Indian History*, vol. XLIV, pt. I, (April, 1966) , 31; *Indian Archaeology*, 1965-66 *A Review*, (cyclostyled copy), 40; Krishna Kumar, 'The Lithic Tool Industries of Khajuraho' *Proceedings of the 55th. Indion Science Congress*, (Calcutta, 1968), 533.

[5] The terminology recommended by the Committee apointed by the Section I of the Inernattional Conference on Asian Archaeology, 1961, together with that recently suggested by Prof. H. D. Sankalia, in his presidential address to the First Annual Meeting of the Archaeological Society of India held at Varanasi on 23rd. February, 1968, has been adopted in this paper.

[6] The Archaeological significance of the river-crossings has already been shown by Drs. R. and B. Allchin in their paper 'The Archaeology of a River-crossing', published in *Indian Anthropology–Essays in the memory of D.N. Majumdar*, (Bombay, 1962), pp. 52 ff.

[7] A group of chisel holes was observed on one of the outcrops near the old road (shown with dotted lines on the map; fig. 1), although their real significance is not known, they appear to have been left over by the stone diggers, who are often active there.

[8] D. H. Gordon, *Prehistoric Background of Indian, Culture*, (Bombay, 1958), 18.

[8a] Though it is a modern construction, which houses some fragmentary sculptures of Chandella period, yet it probably also perpetuates an old site of the cult of Mother-goddess, which had a wide prevalence in the neolithic society. Cf. D. D. Kosambi, *An Introduction to the Study of Indian History*, (Bombay, 1956), 31-46.

[9] Similar pattern has also been noticed at Birbhanpur. Cf. B. B. Lal, 'Birbhanpur: A Microlithic Site in Damodar Valley, West Bengal,' *Ancient India*, No. 14, (195), 14.

[10] A big flatish oval granite pebble; a single flake scar on its lower end results in a straight edge.

[11] A small limestone flake; two shallow flake scars on left side of the dorsal surface and a limited retouch on the right ventral margin form the working edge, with a 'S' twist. The lower tip is damaged presumbly due to its use; it could have served as a side scraper also.

[12] *Indian Archaeology*, 1955-56 *A Review*,40; (1956-57),. 15 & 79; 14 (1957-58), 26; (1958-59), 26, (1959 60), 46-48; (1960-61), 62; (1961-62), 24, 54, 100; (1962-63), 32, 37, 39, 49, 88 & 89; D. H. Gordon, 'The Stone Industries of the Holocene in India and Pakistan' *Ancient India*, No. 6, (1950), 65; Allchin (1959), *op. cit*, 104, Joshi, *op. cit.*, 5ff; Sankalia, *Prehistory and Protohistory in India and Pakistan*, (Bombay, 1963), 140 ff.

[13] *Indian Archaeology*, 1964-65, *A Review*, (cyclostyled copy), 2, etc.

[14] R. E. M. Wheeler, *Early India and Pakistan*, (London, 1959), 137.

[15] M. G. Dikshit, *Tripuri*—1952, (Nagpur, 1955).

[16] Gordon, (1950), *op. cit*, 64 ff.

[17] Gordon, (1958), *op. cit.*, 19-21.

[18] The arrow-heads with pronounced tang or antennae seems to have evolved from points with incipient tang or notch for hafting.

[19] This tool-type may be compared with the remaining tool (type IV B) of Maski. Cf. B. K. Thapar, "Maski A Chalcolithic Site of the Southern Deccan,' *Ancient India*, No. 13, (1957), 91 and 97.

[19 a] Similar beads have been reported from the microlithic sites of Bombay. Cf. K. R. U. Todd, 'The Microlithic Industries of Bombay', *Ancient India*, No 6, (1950), 7.

[20] J. Cockburn, 'On the flint implements from the Kon ravines of South Mirzapur,' *Journal of Royal Asiatic Society of Bengal*, LXIII, pt. iii, (1894), 331-36; Brown, *op. cit.* 70 ff.; *Indian Archaeology*, 1955-56—*A Review*, 41; (1959-60), 48; (1961-62), 54; (1963-64), 43:

[21] See U. V. Singh in *Indian Prehistory*: 1964 (Poona, 1965), 230.

[22] Wheeler, 'Brahmagiri and Chandravalli (1947)', *Ancient India*, No. 4, (1947-48), 180-130.

[23] B. Subbarao, *The Stone Age Cultures of Bellary*, (Poona, 1948), 9.

[24] F. R. Allchin, *Piklihal Excavations*, (Hydrabad, 1960).

[25] K. V. Soundara Rajan, 'Studies in the Stone Age of Nagarjunakonda and its neighbourhood' *Ancient India*, No. 14 (1958), 49-113.

[26] M. S. Nagraja Rao, *The Stone Age Hill Dwellers of Tekkalakota*, (Poona, 1965), 55-68.

[27] A H. Dani, *Prehistory and Protohistory of Eastern India*, (Calcutta, 1960); V.D. Krishnaswami, 'The Neolithic Pattern of India', *Ancient India*, No. 16 (1960), 51 ff.; M. Chakrabarti, 'Occurrence of Neolithic Implements in West Bengal', *Bulletin of Cultural Research Institute*, No. 1&2 (1967), 89. ff.

[28] As these stray finds were obtained one each from the adjoining rain-gulley and a distant cultivated field, it is very likely that the factory site near Jaṭkarā was some sort of living place of the neolithic folk, who practised a primitive cultivation in the fields along the river course.

[29] The first find of a neolith at Khajurāho was made by Major General Cunningham in 1855. It is a small celt (hoe) made on fine trap;, with sharp truncated broken butt, one face is ground flat, Cf. Brown *op. cit.*

[30] Although both the artefacts are devoid of ground and polished edge, these could have been used as hoes or mattocks, which did not require a sharp cutting edge. (Cf. Gordon (1950), *op. cit.*, 79). They may be compared with the adze—*cum*-hoe discovered at Chandolī and similar other finds from Assam. Cf. S.B. Deo and Z. D. Ansari, *Chalcolithic Chandoli* (Poona, 1965), 31, fig. 18, no. 3.

[31] The stone vases have been reported from Santhāl Parganā, Mehī and Mohenjodaro in Indo-Pakistan sub-continent, and several prehistoric sites in western Asia. Cf. R.C.P. Singh, 'Stone vases from the Santhal pargana', *Patna University Journal*, vol. XX, No 1, (January, 1965), 152 ff.

[32] Except a small lump of lead obtained from the surface at Locality B, no metal was found from any site. Although in view of the inadequate field work, this point cannot be stressed, still as this sub-continent has never witnessed complete uniformity in its cultural pattern, it is not necessary that we get all the concomitants of the neolithic-chalcolithic culture at Khajurāho too.

[33] See D.P. Agrawal in *Indian Prehistory : 1964*, 140 & 200, *Indian Archaeology, 1967-68 A Review* p. 70

[34] U. V. Singh, *op. cit.*, 30.

[35] Sir Mortimer Wheeler has rightly remarked "In Central India, it would seem that the stone axes were superimposed upon, or commingled with the microlithic flake industries which were already rooted in the centre and south of the subcontinent." Cf. Wheeler, *op cit.*, 91.

[36] True Early Stone Age industry has not yet been discovered at Khajurāho. Since it has already been reported from elsewhere in the neighbourhood (cf. *Indian-Archaeology*, 1960-61 *A Review*, 59), it is very likely that, if this area is explored further, definite evidences of that industry may be obtained here also.

[37] Sankalia (1962), *op. cit.*, 239.

[38] E. C. Warman, Jr., 'The "neolithic" problem in the Prehistory of India', *Journal of Washington Academy of Sciences*, XXXIX, (1942), 118-20.

[39] Dani, *op. cit.*, 81.

[40] Sankalia (1962), *op. cit.*, 154.

[41] Krishnaswami, *op. cit.*, 28.

[42] B. K. Thapar, 'The Neolithic Problem in India', *Indian Prehistory : 1964*, 68.

[43] See G. C. Mohapatra in *Indian Prehistory : 1964*, 79.

[44] As Dr. B. B. Lal, Chief Archaeological Chemist, Archaeological Survey of India, Dehradun, has kindly agreed to undertake a geochronological survey of the stone age sites of Khajuraho, his study is expected to throw welcome light on the environmental conditions and the dates of various lithic industries of this area.

A Note on makar Figurines

by T. N. Roy

Among the major groups of animals represented in Indian Art and Archaeology, the "crocodilians" number fewer than any other, yet these are depicted on pottery, sculptures, amulets and terracotta plaques. It is not surprising that in such a small assemblage there is not much difference in the general appearance of individual species [1]. Apparently the specimens studied by me appear to be the *Gavialis Gangeticus,* the only Indian crocodile inhabiting the Ganga and its tributaries even today [2]. The important ancient sites yielding such figured materials are Hastinapura, Kausambi, Rajghat, Vaisali and Kumrahar in the Ganga valley and Nagarjunakonda and Nevasa outside the valley.

The most distinctive figure of a *makar-mukha* appears in the Ganga valley round about the early centuries of the Christian era. The examples are from Rajghat and Hastinapura, the one situated on the bank of the Ganga and the other on its tributary, the *Kali-nadi.* The depiction is on a spout which bears at the luting point a decorative moulded design of a *makar-mukha,* i. e. a crocodile figurine. The earliest Rajghat specimen is from the top level of Period II dated from 2nd century B. C. to the beginning of the christian era, but at Hastinapura it is from the mid-level of Period IV dated from the early 2nd century B. C. to late 3rd century A. D. [3]. Similar spouts have also been reported from Kumrahar (Pl. VI, No 4) [4] and Vaisali [5] (Pl. VI, No. 5), Periods III dated from C. 100 to 300 A.D. But at Rajghat (Pl. VI, No. 3) these spouts become fairly common in Period III dated from O to 300 A.D. but in Period IV dated from 300 A. D. to 700 A.D., their frequency is less and the figurines become rough and conventionalized as compared to the preceding periods [6].

The depiction of the animal, particularly its head on the spout and its provenance only in the Ganga valley is not without significance. Giants among the reptiles, the crocodiles are the aquatic animals and the great importance of water to the crocodilian is shown by the shape and form of its head. It is the head which concentrates immediate attention as it remains above the water when the animal floats. And zoologically the only Indian crocodile called the *Gavialis Gangeticus* is also found in northern India confined mostly to the Ganga.

From a single Rajghat specimen, where the *makar-mukha* spout is found fixed to a complete red ware vase decorated on the body with a row of stamped *Triratna* symbol and a panel of petal like design, it appears that these vessels were used for ceremonial or ritualistic purposes.

The depiction of crocodiles also continued in other forms. In one of the interesting sculptures of a Bharhut stone railing on the obverse we find a *makar* figure (Pl. VI, No. 2) along with an inscription [7]. In another sculpture of the Sunga period acquired by the Allahabad museum from Kausambi (Pl. VI, No. 1), we get the crocodile motif on a stone cross-bar [8]. In the excavations at Nagarjunakonda, a terracotta plaque representing *makar-knṇḍalas* has been reported along with other terracotta collections [9]. As far as Nevasa is concerned, the *makar*-amulets (Pl. VI, No. 6) of terracotta have been reported in the early part of the Christian era [12]. As a part of ornaments its depiction continued as late as Gupta period. In one of the Vishṇu sculptures from Mathura belonging to the Gupta period, we find the representaion of two *makar-mukhas* in an ornament which is used as a head dress [11].

Notes

[1] The identification of species on the basis of their depiction on the varied materials in Indian Art will not be desirable to the students of archaeology as this will result in too much of zoological technicalities. This can, however, be done when more material from other Indian sites is presented. For the time being the paper may serve to stimulate more work in this direction.

[2] H. pope Clifford, *The Reptile World*, 43 and R. L. Ditmans, *Reptiles of the World*, 9.

[3] *A. I.* Nos 10 and 11, 71, pl. xxxii, 17.

[4] *Kumrahar Excavations*, 76.

[5] *Vaisali Excavations*, 49.

[6] On my own study of Rajghat material due to the courtesy of Prof. A. K. Narain.

[7] *I.A.*, 1959-60, 82 and *I. A.* 1960-61, 74.

[8] *I.A.*, 1959-60, 76.

[9] *I.A.*, 1956-57, 38.

[10] *I.A.*, 1960-61, 21.

[11] V. S. Agrawal, *Harsha-Charita*, 14.

Chronology of the Indian Megaliths—Some Considerations

by K. S. RAMACHANDRAN

Over a stretch of a century and a half innumerable megaliths have been excavated. Recently, a few habitational sites of this culture, particularly at Brahmagiri and Maski, have also been tackled. While the burials and the habitational vestiges have brought to light the varied cultural milieu of the megalithic complex, attempts at dating the burials have been fraught with difficulties and tend towards approximation only. This is so, even after the recent radiocarbon dating innovation. In this paper it is proposed to review the dates so far obtained through the conventional sequence dating methods and radiocarbon dates.

Conventional sequence datings

1. Wheeler's excavation at Brahmagiri, by far the most scientifically excavated megalithic site, has given a date-range of *C.* 200 B. C.-A. D. 50 for this culture [1]. In arriving at this date-range his considerations were :

(i) On the lower side, the earlier stone-axe culture represented by a late urn-burial overlapped into the earliest layers of the succeeding megalithic culture;

(ii) the terminal date was fixed by the commencement of the Andhra Culture, dated on the basis of Roman coins, Rouletted Ware sherds, etc.; and

(iii) the duration of the megalithic culture was determined by the 3-4 feet of habitational accumulation of the megalithic culture for which he has allowed a conservative time-lapse of nearly two centuries.

This date-range is equally applied to the burials, for Wheeler found identical ceramic types, numbering fourteen, both in the burials and habitation; 'the commonest of them being tulip-shaped vases, carinated bowls, dishes with incurved rims and bowls [2]. This became the sheet-anchor for later excavators for dating the burials.

2. Rea found seventeen urn-burials below a subsidiary *stupa* at Amaravati which in relation to the main *stupa* has been dated to *C.* 200 B. C. [3]. But a reassessment on stylistic grounds of the sculptures found here and the discovery of remnants of an Asokan pillar the date of the main *stupa* has to be pushed back still earlier and consequently that of the burials too.

3. From a cist-grave at Sulur in the Coimbatore district, Tamil Nadu, a bronze coin was obtained which Allan has identified as 'Eran struck' coin minted between C. third-second century B. C. [4].

4. A coin of the Roman emperor Augustus (27 B. C. —A. D. 14) was found from a megalithic grave in Coimbatore district[5].

5. A gold coin, probably a Roman Aureues issued from Constantinople and assignable to the fourth century A. D. was found from a barrow in the Nilgiris[6].

Thus we have a date-range between third century B. C. or a little earlier and the fourth century A. D.

Radiocarbon dates

The following are the available radiocarbon dates :

Site	TF no.	Age (half value 5730)	Dates
Bainapalle (Paiyampalli)	350	2330±105	380 B.C. [7]
Halingali	685	2030±100	80 B.C. [8]
Hallur	573	2905±100	955 B.C. [9]
	570	3055±105	1105 B.C.
Kakoria	179	200± 95	1750 A.D.[10]
Kotia	318	225±100	1725 A.D.[11]
	319	2200±105	250 B.C.
	320	490±100	1460 A.D.
	321	995±100	955 A.D.
	322	490±100	1460 A.D.

Of these, excepting two, one from Halingali TF 685) and the other from Kotia (TF 319), the rest are from habitation sites.

Date samples TF 318, 320–322, all irom Kotia, and TF 179 pertaining to Kakoria, need not be considered, since, according to the dating laboratory, the samples were found contaminated; consequently give late reckoning. Further, the dates run beyond the tenth century, by which time, excepting for the atrophied megalithism in the form of *Viragals* which persisted until recent times and those of the tribal regions of eastern India, mega—lithism as such in India had died out.

Thus we are left with Paiyampalli, Halingali, Hallur and a sample (TF 319) from Kotia.

1. Paiyampalli–TF 350–charred grain—date-range 380±105 B. C.

This pertains to the Black-and-red ware iron culture; the dated sample coming from the habitation site. This habitation site has been linked to the burials excavated in the same place through identical pottery types, such as tulip-shaped vases in Black-and-red ware, funnel-shaped lids in all-black ware, ring-stands of the hour-glass type and three-legged jars in red ware. All these shapes, particularly the three-legged jars and the funnel-shaped lids are typical of the megalithic burials of the peninsular region. Further, they compare well with the Brahmagiri types.

2. Halingali-TF685-charcoal date-range 80±100 B. C.

The sample is drawn from the burial itself and the date-range is well within the time bracket observed elsewhere.

3. Kotia-TF 319–charcoal date-range250± 100 B. C. The remarks regarding Halingali are applicable to this site as well.

Hallur-TF 570 and 573-charcoal date-range 1105±105 B. C. and 955±100 B. C. respectively.

These two dated samples of the neolithic-megalithic overlap phase came from the habitation site. Both the samples are from the same trench (Trench 1); the former from layer 4 and the latter from layer 5 at a depth ranging from 1.80–2.10 m and 2.35–3.55 m. respectively. The earlier date is afforded by TF 570, the later by TF 573. These require careful consideration.

(i) It is rather strange that a sample from a later stratum (layer 4) gives an earlier date than the sample from an earlier stratum (layer 5); the difference being a century and a half. This is incompatible with the principles of dating on the basis of stratigraphy. In this light how far these dates could be valid is a moot question.

(ii) Although nearabout the habitation area megalithic burials were noticed, unfortunately none of them was excavated. Thus the habitation and the burials remain unconnected.

(iii) The brief notice of the excavation in *Indian Archaealogy 1964-65* (under print) does not mention the pottery from the habitation area; thus depriving their being linked with the known pottery shapes from similar burials elsewhere.

In the absence of indisputable connecting link as in the case of Brahmagiri or Paiyampalli, it would be hazardous to accept these dates for the burials as well. At best these could be considered applicable to the habitational strata and for Black-and-red ware and iron in this region. It would not be tenable to assume that Black-and-red ware plus iron ushered in the megalithic mode of burial, for all that we know the megalithic folk from their region of dispersal into India did not bring with them these two cultural items, but assimilated them as part of their cultural and burial-complex; thus their coming is posterior to Black-and-red ware and iron, for, according to the present day evidence, megalithic monuments and related habitational strata, all belong to Iron Age complex.

Interesting sidelight of these dates for iron, one of which is earlier than Atranjikhera [12] (1025+110 B.C.) would warrant a postulation of a bi-pronged diffusion of this metal into India; one from the north and the other from a place of contact on the west coast.

CONCLUSIONS

1. Conventional methods give a date-range from third century B. C. or a little earlier to fourth century A. D.

2. Radiocarbon dates of Paiyampalli, Kotia and Halingali give a central date-range well within the fourth century B. C. for the earlier side.

3. Radiocarbon dates from Hallur are open to question for (i) they pertain to habitational area unlinked with the burials through common bonds, and (ii) the dates themselves are incompatible with and against the accepted principles of dating through stratigraphical sequence.

4. Iron diffused into India from two points, one from the north and the other from a point of contact on the west coast.

Notes

[1] R. E. M. Wheeler, 'Brahmagiri and Chandravalli 1947 : Megalithic and other Civilizations, Mysore State', *Ancient India*, No. 4, 1948, 200-202.

[2] *Ibid.*, 232,

[3] Alexander Rea, 'Excavations at Amaravati', *Annual Report of the Archaeological Survey of India* 1908-09, (Calcutta), 1912, 88-91.

[4] Horace C. Beck, 'Notes on Sundry Asiatic Beads', *Man*, XXX, 1930, Art. No. 134.

[5] 'Early Roman intercourse with India', *Indian Antiquary*, II, 1873, 241—42.

[6] J. Hough, *Letters on the Climate etc., of the Neilgherries*, (London), 1879, 8-84 as quoted by Banerjee in *Ancient India*, No. 9.

[7] D. P. Agrawal, *et al.*, 'Radiocarbon dates of samples from Southern Neolithic sites'. *Current Science*, 35, No. 23, 1966, 585-86

[8] *Indian Archaeology—1967-68 A Review*, 71

[9] Agrawal, *op. cit.* for Hallur dates.

[10] Agrawal, *et al. op. cit.*, 35, No. 1, 1966, 4-5.

[11] Agrawal, reprint of Radiocarbon dates.

[12] Agrawal, *et al. op. cit.*, 33, No. 9. 1964, 266-69.